CONVERSION WORKS

Conversion Works

Jeffrey A. Allen

CASCADE *Books* · Eugene, Oregon

CONVERSION WORKS

Cascade Books
An Imprint of Wipf and Stock Publishers
199 W. 8th Ave., Suite 3
Eugene, OR 97401

www.wipfandstock.com

PAPERBACK ISBN: 978-1-5326-8876-8
HARDCOVER ISBN: 978-1-5326-8877-5
EBOOK ISBN: 978-1-5326-8878-2

Cataloguing-in-Publication data:

Names: Allen, Jeffrey A.
Title: Conversion works / Jeffrey A. Allen.
Description: Eugene, OR: Cascade Books, 2021 | Includes bibliographical references.
Identifiers: ISBN 978-1-5326-8877-5 (paperback) | ISBN 978-1-5326-8877-5 (hardcover) | ISBN 978-1-5326-8878-2 (ebook)
Subjects: LCSH: Philosophers—Biography—History and criticism. | Conversion—History.
Classification: B104 .A48 2021 (print) | B104 (ebook)

Contents

Introduction

IN THIS BOOK, CONVERSION means abandoning a world view and starting over.[1] Using this definition of conversion, the book examines four works: Augustine of Hippo's *Confessions* (c. 401 AD), René Descartes's *Meditations on First Philosophy* (1641), Bernard Lonergan's *Insight: A Study of Human Understanding* (1957), and Peter Weir's *The Truman Show* (1998). The first three works are books; the fourth work is a film. The main argument of this book is that all four works contain and induce conversion. That is, all four works feature an individual who abandons a world view and starts over, and all four works exhort their engager to do the same. To clarify the terms: a world view is an overarching conception of reality, and to start over means to exhibit a full acceptance of the implications of world view-abandonment.

The title of this book, *Conversion Works*, aims to convey that what is being considered is a class of works. What this book takes to warrant belonging to the class is not only the containment and induction of conversion; cognitive imitation and private engagement must also play a role in the work. Cognitive imitation involves the reader or viewer replicating the mental activities of the individual who has a conversion in the work; private engagement involves reading or viewing the work while alone. The degree and manner of both cognitive imitation and private engagement vary from work to work. The most substantial variation relates to *The*

---

1. This definition is adapted from Paul S. MacDonald. See MacDonald, "Philosophical Conversion," 304.

Truman Show—specifically, its manner of private engagement. Weir could not require his film to be engaged while alone given that its initial venue was the movie theater. Nevertheless, the film is designed to dissuade interaction with others, especially during the scene that contains and induces conversion. Less substantial variations will be identified when examining a work.

Establishing a class named conversion works in chapters 1 to 4 is necessary before the secondary argument of this book can be made. Chapter 5 argues for the contemporary educational value of the four works under consideration. This secondary argument involves an extensive engagement with cultural anthropologist Ernest Becker's *The Denial of Death*.

That this book's secondary argument is made exclusively in chapter 5 does not mean chapters 1 to 4 are uninfluenced by it. Those chapters intentionally supply a wealth of explanatory quotations from scholars that educators can appropriate. This book has indeed been written with educators in mind. However, any person seeking deeper insight into one or more of the works considered will hopefully be able to benefit from this book. In fact, the book has been composed such that persons can skip one or more chapters depending on their interests. Some comparative analysis is unavoidable and some is too illuminating to pass over, but it is never so substantial as to require one to read more than one chapter. What cannot be skipped, by educators and non-educators alike, is reading the portion of a work that holds the arc of conversion before reading its respective chapter in this book. One needs to have read Book VII of the *Confessions* before reading chapter 1, the First and Second Meditation in the *Meditations* before chapter 2, and chapters 1 to 11 of *Insight* before chapter 3. The outlier here is *The Truman Show*; since the arc of conversion spans the entire film, it needs to be viewed from beginning to end before reading chapter 4.

The structure of chapters 1 to 4 of this book is, with minor exceptions, as follows: The first section provides a short biography of the creator of the work—except in chapter 4, as will be explained shortly. Biographical details are provided only up to the year in which the work was published. Since the individual who undergoes conversion in each written work is a kind of idealized version of its author, only those details of the author's life that could be infused into the work are relevant. The next section defends the categorization of the work as a conversion work. The moment(s) in which conversion is contained and induced in the work will be identified here. The reason for the plural alternative, moments, is that in the *Meditations* there is a slight separation between the containment and induction of conversion. The sections following this highlight the roles of cognitive imitation and private engagement. The final section, which is the longest section in each chapter, provides a map of conversion in the work. As noted above, one exception to this structure occurs in chapter 4; it does not commence with a biography since the individual who has a conversion in *The Truman Show* is neither the creator of the work, nor an idealized version of the creator, but a fictional character. Another exception occurs in chapter 3, on *Insight*, which partially maps conversion before highlighting the roles of cognitive imitation and private engagement; it then returns to the mapping.

Time must be taken now to address a similarity between the works that rests beyond the four elements of a conversion work—beyond containing conversion, inducing conversion, featuring cognitive imitation, and featuring private engagement. As it happens, materialism is abandoned in all four works. Materialism is a world view that takes the real to be fundamentally material. The phrase "as it happens" aims to avoid any sense that the works were chosen because they abandon materialism—or that this book seeks to undermine materialism. The works were chosen because they share the four elements listed above. But a question remains: if conversion means abandoning a world view, and if the materialist world view is abandoned in all four works, why not designate the abandonment of *materialism* as an element of conversion works? The answer is that the four works vary in terms of their treatment of materialism, including whether it is marked as problematic at the outset and how clearly it is marked as unviable at the end of the arc of conversion. In the *Meditations*, for example, the world known via the attitude of unsophisticated empiricism is Descartes's root concern; when he discounts that attitude at the end of the Second Meditation, he does so on a basis that renders materialism unviable. Here, and even in the other three works, abandoning the world view of materialism is too programmatically varied to be deemed a requisite element of a conversion work.[2]

Yet another preliminary note is needed regarding how the works themselves are analyzed in this book. Chapters 1 to 4 endeavor to interpret the works under consideration without reference to other works by the same creator.[3] This approach respects the fact that the works, in their creators' minds, offer everything needed for the induction of conversion. An additional way in which the four works are respected as stand-alone texts is through the aforementioned avoidance of comparative analysis. But it must be stressed that this avoidance does not mean there are no comparative paths worth exploring. Several such paths have been explored,[4] and there are more that await exploration. To give just one example, there is the significant role played by women in raising the authors of the first three works. Augustine lost his father, whom he does not appear to have been close to, while a teenager; he and his siblings were subsequently raised by their mother, Monica.[5] Descartes was similarly not very close to his father, who was often away from home; he and his siblings were raised mainly by his maternal grandmother, Jeanne Sain, and a nurse.[6] Finally, Lonergan's father was also regularly away from home, for work; he and his siblings were primarily raised by their mother, Josephine,

2. An additional reason for refraining from deeming it essential is outside the scope of this book but worth identifying: the possibility of a conversion *to* materialism. On this possibility, see MacDonald, "Philosophical Conversion," 307; and Riley, *Character and Conversion*, 7.

3. Unavoidably, some secondary materials that are utilized offer insights that stem from an examination of early or later works by a creator.

4. For example, Menn, *Descartes and Augustine*; and Riley, *Character and Conversion*, both of which this book appeals to.

5. Chadwick, *Augustine*, 7 and 11.

6. Clarke, *Descartes*, 9–10. Descartes's mother, Jeanne, passed away a year after giving birth to him.

and her sister, Mary.[7] It is hoped that this book inspires an investigation of this and other intriguing common threads.

The remainder of this introduction unpacks what is meant by the term *conversion*. The definition of conversion employed in this book, namely, abandoning a world view and starting over, is adapted from philosopher Paul S. MacDonald. For MacDonald, to have a "philosophical conversion" is "to abandon a philosophical world-view and to begin again from the ground up."[8] Although this book is greatly indebted to MacDonald, there was a need for both a revised term and a revised description that could be applied to all four works under consideration. For different reasons, these revisions require justification.

To speak of conversion instead of philosophical conversion requires justification, for scholars have in fact used the latter term in relation to the authors treated in this book. Philosophers Stephen Menn and Carl Vaught do so with Augustine;[9] MacDonald and languages scholar Patrick Riley do so with Descartes;[10] and theologian William Mathews does so with Lonergan.[11] Philosophical conversion does not, however, appear to have ever been invoked in relation to Weir. This is somewhat to be expected, given the medium of his work. By contrast, conversion has been employed in relation to Weir by theologian Richard Leonard.[12] Leonard's use of conversion and his related reflections on *The Truman Show* have

7. Mathews, *Lonergan's Quest*, 19.

8. MacDonald, "Philosophical Conversion," 304. Hyphen in the original.

9. Menn, *Descartes and Augustine*, 204n51; Vaught, *Encounters with God*, 1.

10. MacDonald, "Philosophical Conversion," 304; Riley, *Character and Conversion*, 73.

11. Mathews, *Lonergan's Quest*, 204. It is worth noting here that other scholars have invoked the term. Stanley Cavell, for example, reports having undergone a "philosophical conversion" himself. Italianist Matteo Soranzo and historian Denis Robichaud, to give another example, find in Plato and Plotinus a "language of philosophical conversion." Conant, "Interview with Stanley Cavell," 44; and Soranzo and Robichaud, "Philosophical or Religious Conversion?," 144.

12. Leonard, "Mystical Gaze," 55, 70, and 279.

much in common with the phenomenon that the scholars above point to in their writing—enough that revising philosophical conversion is preferable to replacing it with a more general term, such as transformation. The term conversion allows *The Truman Show*—and potentially other films—to be examined alongside the work of thinkers like Augustine, Descartes, and Lonergan.

To speak of abandoning a world view instead of abandoning a philosophical world view also requires justification. The decision stems from the fact that all four works seek to reach the general public. Now, the three written works are indeed tailored to satisfy the expectations and anticipate the objections of the scholarly community, which includes philosophers. Nevertheless, all four works explicitly or implicitly deem members of both communities to be in need of the same conversion. The decision, then, acknowledges the non-scholar who engages one of the works and abandons materialism without knowing it to be an established philosophical world view. The decision also facilitates the aim of chapter 5, where the educational value of all four works will be discussed from a wide angle that includes but is not limited to philosophy courses.

To speak of starting over instead of beginning again from the ground up is the last item requiring justification. While MacDonald's description certainly applies to the *Meditations*, towards which he invokes it, it does not apply to the *Confessions*, *Insight*, or *The Truman Show*. The revised expression, starting over, applies to all four works. Now, it was stated earlier that starting over means exhibiting a full acceptance of the implications of world view-abandonment. The way the four creators exhibit this in their works varies substantially and is best left to the chapters that follow. What is common, however, is a shift in which the roles of cognitive imitation and private engagement are minimized or removed.

One last introductory note must be made. Conversion, as this book envisions it, owes a great debt not only to MacDonald but also to Riley. Focusing on autobiographical works, Riley describes conversion as "the foundational moment in which [an autobiographer] adopts a new philosophical system, worldview, or vocation."[13] This description supports linking conversion with a change of world view. Riley employs the description in his analysis of the *Confessions*, as well as in his analysis of Descartes's 1637 work *Discourse on the Method*—a work with connections to the *Meditations*.[14] Riley also highlights a kind of starting over in the *Confessions* and the *Discourse*: "both . . . renounce autobiographical narrative in the wake of radical change."[15]

At the same time, Riley's overall approach to conversion differs from that of this book. As hinted at in the description above, Riley attends to the new world view adopted after conversion. Moreover, Riley examines both the "preconversional and postconversional selves" on display in the works that he examines.[16] This book, by contrast, does not investigate the new world view adopted or the postconversional self that carries out the adoption.

Perhaps the best way to distinguish this book is to restate its rationale in a single sentence. A class named conversion works has been proposed to recognize and inspect in a similar way four works that share four elements: the containment of conversion, the induction of conversion, cognitive imitation, and private engagement.

---

13. Riley, *Character and Conversion*, 2.

14. The *Discourse on the Method* contains autobiographical and programmatic overlap with the *Meditations*. One might take this to imply that reflections on the former work could be transferred over to the latter; however, the difference in the meaning of conversion and contrasting attitude towards imitation in the two works precludes such an approach.

15. Riley, *Character and Conversion*, 74.

16. Riley, *Character and Conversion*, 16.

1

Conversion in Book VII
of Augustine of Hippo's *Confessions*

Background

AUGUSTINE WAS BORN ON November 13, 354 in the town of Thagaste (present-day Souk Ahras, Algeria). In adulthood, he would become bishop of Hippo (present-day Annaba, Algeria), thus he is typically referred to in English as Augustine of Hippo. Augustine's parents, Patrick and Monica, owned farmland and were of modest economic standing.[1] Patrick was a pagan; Monica was a devout Christian. Patrick died in 372, converting to Christianity on his deathbed.

Around the time his father died, Augustine went away to Carthage for the present-day equivalent of university. While there, he read Cicero's *Hortensius*, which warns that happiness is found in the pursuit of truth rather than in the pursuit of pleasure.[2] This raised deep philosophical and religious questions in Augustine's mind.[3] Having attended church with Monica, the answers provided by the Bible were known to Augustine, but they did not

---

1. Chadwick, Introduction to *Confessions*, xiii.
2. Chadwick, Introduction to *Confessions*, xiii–xiv.
3. Chadwick, *Augustine*, 11.

intellectually satisfy him.[4] At Carthage, Augustine was also exposed to Manichaeism, a relatively new religion. Manichaeism stemmed from Mani, who was born c. 216 in Babylonia. As Kevin Coyle explains, Mani believed that "previous revelations from God, especially to Buddha, Zoroaster, and Jesus [were] authentic but incomplete"—and that he should "bring divine revelation in full to the world."[5] Manichees held that a battle between light and darkness was being waged throughout the universe. The victory of the light would come in part through the denial of human pleasure, thus Manichaeism had a certain affinity to the warning of Cicero in *Hortensius*. Augustine eventually joined the religion as a Hearer. A Hearer had fewer strictures than the Elect; for example, a Hearer could marry, whereas the Elect could not.[6] Augustine would remain a Hearer for nine years—specifically, from the ages of nineteen to twenty-eight.[7]

Augustine commenced a teaching career in 375 that included literature, rhetoric, and dialectic. He taught in his birthplace of Thagaste, as well as in Carthage, Rome, and Milan. When he arrived in Milan in 384, his belief in Manichaeism had significantly waned; this opened up the possibility of conversion.[8] At this crucial juncture, Augustine met Ambrose, the bishop of Milan. Ambrose appropriated elements of Neoplatonism into his preaching and put the Bible in a new light for Augustine.[9] Peter Brown holds that it is hard to determine the precise level of Ambrose's influence on what this book refers to as Augustine's conversion.[10] What is clear is that Ambrose bolstered Augustine's decision to give Christianity a new hearing.[11] The ultimate outcome of that new hearing was an affirmation of Christianity in 386 and baptism by Ambrose in 387.

4. Chadwick, *Augustine*, 11–12.

5. Coyle, *Manichaeism and its Legacy*, xiii.

6. Chadwick, *Augustine*, 12.

7. Starnes, *Augustine's Conversion*, 73.

8. Chadwick, Introduction to *Confessions*, xix.

9. Chadwick, Introduction to *Confessions*, xxi.

10. Brown, *Augustine of Hippo*, 76.

11. Brown, *Augustine of Hippo*, 77.

Monica, who had hoped for this moment for so long, passed away not long after it occurred. In 391 Augustine was ordained a priest. The details of his ordination are startling to our sensibilities today. While Augustine was attending Sunday church service, Valerius, bishop of Hippo, said that he was in need of a new priest and that Augustine would be good for the role.[12] This did not result in a long period of reflection by Augustine. Instead, as Henry Chadwick writes, ordination was "forced upon [him] by the coercion of the congregation. Augustine was allowed no escape, and had to submit."[13] Bishop Valerius also wanted to ensure that Augustine would remain in Hippo, thus he persuaded an official to make Augustine coadjutor bishop of Hippo in 395. Within two years, Bishop Valerius had died; Augustine took over, and he would remain bishop of Hippo until the end of his life.[14]

Augustine likely began writing the *Confessions* in 397; it appears to have been completed in 401.[15] As announced at the outset of this book, Augustine's post-*Confessions* life will not be reviewed in detail. It can simply be stated that Augustine went on to compose several writings against views already or ultimately deemed heretical, including Donatism, Pelagianism, Arianism, and paganism. He also composed a unique work, entitled *Retractions*, a few years before passing away. In this work, he looks back on his writings chronologically and carries out both self-criticism and self-explanation.[16] After falling ill with a fever, Augustine died on August 28, 430.[17]

---

12. Chadwick, Introduction to *Confessions*, xi.

13. Chadwick, Introduction to *Confessions*, xi.

14. Brown, *Augustine of Hippo*, 132–33.

15. Quinn, *Companion to the "Confessions,"* 10n2.

16. Brown, *Augustine of Hippo*, 433.

17. Brown, *Augustine of Hippo*, 436.

The *Confessions* as a Conversion Work

It should be immediately clarified that by "confessions" Augustine means not only admittance of failure—the primary meaning of the term today—but also admittance of praise.[18] When one is conscious of the latter, it comes as less of a surprise to learn that the entire work is addressed to God. Augustine has various means to communicate this, from starting chapters with "Lord" to his regular use of the phrase "I confess to you."

Augustine's *Confessions* consists of thirteen books. Books I to IX of the *Confessions* are autobiographical in character; he treats his life from his birth in 354 to the death of his mother in 387.[19] Apparently completed in 401, the final event covered in the *Confessions* is more than a decade removed and the earliest event covered over forty years removed. In addition to the temporal distance, Augustine did not have his mother or father available to help him recall the past, nor did he have the aid of photographs and video recordings. For these reasons, no one would expect the *Confessions* to be a flawless historical record. What might not occur to the contemporary reader, however, is whether he or she should expect the work to provide a historical record—in the contemporary sense of the term—at all. Carl Vaught describes Augustine as "a rhetorician and a storyteller, living and writing in [an] oral culture."[20] Augustine's venture, he continues, "is not to produce a scientifically accurate account of his experience, but to allow memory, forgetfulness, reconstruction, and providence to interplay with one another to forge the story of a unified life."[21] Even if Augustine was aware of contemporary standards for autobiography, he might still have engaged in reconstruction. As Annemaré Kotzé observes, in Books I to IX Augustine wants to "make explicit . . . the implications his life-story [has] for the reader's own life."[22] This portion of the work

---

18. Chadwick, Introduction to *Confessions*, ix.

19. Vaught, *Encounters with God*, 4.

20. Vaught, *Encounters with God*, 20.

21. Vaught, *Encounters with God*, 20.

22. Kotzé, *Augustine's "Confessions,"* 30.

is tailored, then, for readers' internalization—an internalization that would not occur through the mere presentation of facts. It is this tailoring that also helps one make sense of why Augustine would address an autobiography to God, who in theory already knows every detail of Augustine's life. Augustine lets readers eavesdrop on his prayer to God about his past in the hope that they find it relevant to their own lives. In fact, there is a sense in which the latter cannot but be the case. As Robert McMahon contends, "Every reader impersonates the narrator's 'I' in [Augustine's] dialogue with God. Indeed, every reader necessarily becomes Augustine the narrator making his *Confessions*."²³ McMahon's specification of Augustine the narrator is important and will be addressed shortly.

In Books X to XIII one finds, as Patrick Riley observes, "a metaphysical treatise on memory, temporality, language, and biblical exegesis"²⁴ written in "an analytical, impersonal voice."²⁵ Recalling this book's definition of conversion, namely, to abandon a world view and start over,²⁶ one would expect that starting over occurs in Book X—and it does. What one might also expect is for the abandonment of a world view to occur in Book IX—namely, right before starting over. This is not the case. Augustine's overarching concern in the *Confessions* is religious, thus what prompts the transition from autobiography to treatise, and a starting over, is religious conversion. In Book VIII, Augustine recounts being in a garden in Milan and hearing a nearby voice instruct him, "'Pick up and read, pick up and read.'"²⁷ He interprets this to mean that he should pick up Paul's Letter to the Romans, which he has with him, and read whatever passage he happens to open to. The passage he lands on is Romans 13:13–14, in which Paul advocates

---

23. McMahon, *Medieval Meditative Ascent*, 92.

24. Riley, *Character and Conversion*, 24.

25. Riley, *Character and Conversion*, 26.

26. This definition is adapted from MacDonald, "Philosophical Conversion," 304.

27. Augustine, *Confessions*, 8.12.29. Only internal references are supplied for the *Confessions*; for other works, an external reference is provided first, followed by an internal reference in square brackets.

letting go of lust and aligning oneself with Jesus. Augustine goes on to describe the event as "converting me to [God]," with a resolution to neither "seek a wife" nor have "ambition for success in this world."[28] In Book IX, he discusses his baptism—an ecclesial marker of religious conversion.[29] These are the phenomena that precede starting over. To find the abandonment of a world view, one must look earlier in the work.

It is in Book VII that one finds Augustine abandoning a world view. Through the abandonment, Augustine moves from an inadequate conception of God to an intellectual vision in which he grasps God as God truly is. This event puts him on course for his religious conversion in Book VIII. That is, the conversion of Book VII renders justified and authentic the religious conversion that follows it. The logic in play here discloses the target audience of Book VII as well as the *Confessions* as a whole. As Kotzé claims, it was primarily written for others who have struggled with converting to Catholicism on intellectual grounds—especially the Manichees.[30] The profile is somewhat captured in Augustine's own words at the outset of Book VI: "I was not now a Manichee, though neither was I a Catholic Christian."[31] Kotzé holds that the *Confessions* is written, secondarily, for those who "may already be converted but remain in need of constant encouragement and exhortation."[32]

What Book VII provides across its twenty-one chapters is a report on the development of his view of God that is sympathetic to persons trapped in one or another of the stages of that development. Part of the sympathy can be attributed to self-respect. The conversion that Augustine describes in Book VII seems to have occurred when he was around thirty-two years of age. Passing off the claims of the Manichees as foolish or absurd would lead

28. Augustine, *Confessions*, 8.12.30.

29. On the distance between his affirmation of Christianity and baptism, see O'Donnell, *Augustine*, 60.

30. Kotzé, *Augustine's "Confessions,"* 87–88. See also Brown, *Augustine of Hippo*, 153.

31. Augustine, *Confessions*, 6.1.1.

32. Kotzé, *Augustine's "Confessions,"* 88.

readers to question Augustine's own intelligence and decision-making ability.[33]

By the end of Book VII, it becomes clear that a single philosophical presupposition has been the cause of his incorrect thinking about God. The presupposition is that the real is fundamentally material. Materialism, then, is the world view that Augustine ultimately abandons in Book VII. Importantly, the materialism Augustine subscribed to is not of the kind one would spontaneously think of today; it was not atheistic materialism. Rather, Augustine subscribed to a kind of theistic materialism. To understand this position, one needs to have some familiarity with the Manichaean cosmogony, which is their account of the origin of the universe. As Coyle succinctly explains,

> [Manichaeism] thought of a God of goodness, whose realm was light, and a dark counterpart, whose kingdom was composed of matter. Coeternal, at first the two existed completely apart; but then the evil principle perceived the light, desired it, and invaded it. In the course of the resulting battle, the substance of each became mixed with the other. This is how light and darkness, good and evil, came to form the composition of everything in the present, visible world.[34]

If matter is just as eternal as God, then it is not possible to solve any metaphysical puzzle without referring to matter, especially if the puzzle involves the present world where the two are intermixed. It is this frame of mind that Augustine readopts at the outset of Book VII for the sake of explication. He wants to show that while not formally a Manichee, his thought was still shaped by a philosophical presupposition underlying the Manichaean view of God. It is also possible that it was shaped by a presupposition underlying Christianity, as odd as that initially sounds. John Kenney holds that a kind of materialism may have been present in the Christianity practiced around Augustine, which would explain how he reached his thirties "before encountering the very idea of

33. Chadwick, *Heresy and Orthodoxy*, 204.

34. Coyle, *Manichaeism and its Legacy*, 308–9.

transcendence."[35] The implication of this is that materialism was an unconscious presupposition for Augustine, for he had no alternative to opt for.

It is worth further detailing the battle between light and darkness, including the appearance of human beings in it, for one can gain a sense of how Augustine would have seen his place in the world during his nine years as a Hearer. As Coyle explains,

> To free the light from the matter with which it was now entangled, the God of goodness constructed [celestial bodies] . . . to serve as collector stations for the light eventually freed; they in turn would pass that light back to its true home. To forestall this, the evil principle caused a male and female demon to mate, and their union produced Adam and Eve. They were the world in miniature, since they contained in themselves both light (soul) and matter (body). The first humans, therefore, were not a creation of God, but the consequence of an evil initiative, their sole purpose being to keep as much light entrapped in the visible world as possible, chiefly by generating offspring. . . . Manichaeism called on all humans to remove themselves as far as possible from the consequences of their mixed condition.[36]

The Manichaean belief that Adam and Eve were not created by God is a striking example of how the religion is related to but distinct from Christianity. One ought to appreciate how radical a change it would have been for Augustine to abandon this anthropology, let alone materialism.

Cognitive Imitation

What occurs in Book VII is not a strict argument but a spectacle of reflection that a reader can replicate in his or her own mind. Riley speaks of "the imitative quality of Augustine's conversion"— a conversion that is "an exemplary narrative for other prospective

---

35. Kenney, *Contemplation and Classical Christianity*, 36.
36. Coyle, *Manichaeism and its Legacy*, 309–10. Parentheses in the original.

converts."[37] Kotzé holds that "the reader is . . . made to accompany the young Augustine on every step of the arduous journey."[38] Colin Starnes invokes similar language, stating that the *Confessions* is written "in such a way that we can all follow the path he marked."[39] McMahon contends that Augustine "makes [a] meditative journey, and the reader is . . . involved in it."[40] Another image that can be added here is that of a mountain-climbing guide who has reached the summit of a mountain before and now helps others reach the same place. The image is not perfect, however; in real life, a person can take a helicopter to the summit—but not in the *Confessions*. As John Quinn remarks of Augustine's journey, "[A]t no stage is he borne out of himself or passively penetrated by the presence of God."[41] Overcoming incorrect conceptions of God through imitation occurs incrementally.

An issue related to cognitive imitation that deserves address is just who has a conversion in Book VII. Speaking of the *Confessions* as a whole, McMahon contends that we must distinguish between Augustine the author and Augustine the narrator. He writes, "Augustine the author dramatized, through the voice of his narrator, a process of search and discovery that he had already completed. He dramatized it in a particular way . . . to involve the reader in the drama of Augustine the narrator's quest for truth."[42] Based on McMahon's distinction, it must be clarified that it is Augustine the narrator whom the reader cognitively imitates. Just how much of a gap exists between the historical facts of Augustine's development in his view of God and the development expressed in Book VII can never be fully known.[43]

37. Riley, *Character and Conversion*, 29.

38. Kotzé, *Augustine's "Confessions,"* 216.

39. Starnes, *Augustine's Conversion*, 186.

40. McMahon, *Medieval Meditative Ascent*, 44.

41. Quinn, *Companion to the "Confessions,"* 390.

42. McMahon, *Medieval Meditative Ascent*, 82.

43. McMahon, *Medieval Meditative Ascent*, 83.

Private Engagement

Given the period in which the *Confessions* was written, discussing private engagement involves first a treatment of silent reading and second a treatment of reading while alone. As Paul Saenger asserts, "Ancient reading was usually oral, either aloud, in groups, or individually, in a muffled voice."[44] Evidence of this is found in the *Confessions*. Augustine makes an observation about Ambrose that would be superfluous today: "When he was reading, . . . his voice and tongue were silent."[45] Augustine was impressed by Ambrose's manner of reading. As Margaret Miles explains, Augustine came to realize that "silent reading . . . could penetrate to and reshape the core of his being."[46] Notably, when Augustine obeys the voice saying "Pick up and read," he indicates that he did so "in silence."[47]

Silent reading is one thing; reading alone is another. Garry Wills points out that "[a]ncient readers did not normally read in solitude."[48] It is once again Ambrose that steps outside the norm, for in addition to reading in silence, he also read while alone.[49] Miles asserts that Augustine was impressed by this and began the practice of silent reading while alone.[50]

In light of the above, one imagines Augustine might tailor some of his own writing to be consumed in Ambrose's mode of engagement. According to Miles, Augustine does so with the *Confessions*; he "expected" silent reading while alone.[51]

---

44. Saenger, *Space between Words*, 1.

45. Augustine, *Confessions*, 6.3.3.

46. Miles, "On Reading Augustine," 511.

47. Augustine, *Confessions*, 8.12.29.

48. Wills, *Augustine's "Confessions,"* 5.

49. Miles, "On Reading Augustine," 511.

50. Miles, "On Reading Augustine," 511.

51. Miles, "On Reading Augustine," 512. The opposing view of Leo Ferrari should be acknowledged; he claims that the *Confessions* was meant to be read aloud in front of others. See Ferrari, "Beyond Augustine's Conversion Scene," 102.

A Map of Conversion in the *Confessions*

A term used by Augustine at the outset of Book VII suggests that what he is about to relay pertains to his "early thirties."[52] However, the views he shares represent a long span, from his adoption of Manichaeism to his skepticism about it.[53] As Book VII opens, Augustine recalls being in a personal, philosophical predicament. While he did not think of God as "in the shape of the human body,"[54] he did not know "how otherwise to conceive of [God]."[55] Augustine then isolates the cause of his predicament: he was "unable to think any substance possible other than that which the eyes normally perceive."[56] As a result, he "felt forced to imagine [God as] something physical occupying space diffused either in the world or even through infinite space outside the world."[57] The term "unable" shows that a transformation of thinking is required rather than a mere increase in his body of knowledge.

Augustine states that his "mind's eye," or intellect, was polluted by "physical images"—so much so that, he admits, "I had no clear vision even of my own self."[58] This admission is important inasmuch as it foreshadows a resolution to Augustine's predicament; his mind's eye will somehow no longer be polluted by physical images. Part of the momentum of Book VII, then, comes from the reader's intrigue about how Augustine will become "[uncuffed] from matter-bound thinking,"[59] to borrow from Quinn.

The early sentences of Book VII also serve the project of inducing conversion. Specifically, Augustine's use of "or" in describing how he felt forced to conceive of God establishes the open character of Book VII; it is a spectacle of reflection in which

---

52. Starnes, *Augustine's Conversion*, 27n38. The term is *iuventus*.

53. O'Donnell, "*Confessions*," 392.

54. Augustine, *Confessions*, 7.1.1.

55. Augustine, *Confessions*, 7.1.1.

56. Augustine, *Confessions*, 7.1.1.

57. Augustine, *Confessions*, 7.1.1.

58. Augustine, *Confessions*, 7.1.1–2. He also describes himself as "a man with profound defects." Augustine, *Confessions*, 7.1.1.

59. Quinn, *Companion to the "Confessions*," 341.

multiple angles are considered. By traversing a staggered path, as opposed to a straight one, Augustine frees the reader to tackle other, more personal impediments to clearly conceiving of God.

Augustine next discloses the only kind of substance he thought possible: "I thought simply non-existent anything not extended in space or diffused or concentrated or expanding."[60] In connection with this, he gives a hint of what unimpeded vision of his own self will reveal: "I did not see that the mental power by which I formed [physical] images does not occupy any space."[61] Augustine also shares more detail on the conception of God that he held at this stage: "a large being, permeating infinite space on every side, penetrating the entire mass of the world, and outside this extending in all directions . . . without end."[62] Augustine provides a metaphor of sunlight passing through the air to help the reader grasp his view of God as penetrating everything. The reader naturally wonders how Augustine will ever climb out of this vivid conception. Fortunately, Augustine has a set of beliefs that keep him dissatisfied with the conception. He writes,

> I believed you to be incorruptible, immune from injury, and unchangeable. . . . [I]t was clear to me and certain that what is corruptible is inferior to that which cannot be corrupted; what is immune from injury I unhesitatingly put above that which is not immune; what suffers no change is better than that which can change.[63]

Augustine found this set of beliefs to be in friction with the vivid conception above insofar as there would be "[more of God] in an elephant's body than a sparrow's to the degree that it is larger and occupies more space."[64] As with sunlight, Augustine uses familiar objects so that the reader can join him in the thought experiment. He then relays that he knew he was on the wrong track but had not yet discovered an alternative. The insight that Augustine was

60. Augustine, *Confessions*, 7.1.2.

61. Augustine, *Confessions*, 7.1.2.

62. Augustine, *Confessions*, 7.1.2.

63. Augustine, *Confessions*, 7.1.1.

64. Augustine, *Confessions*, 7.1.2.

missing at this point, as Starnes puts it, was that God and nature are not "composed of the same substance."[65]

What helps Augustine discover an alternative is the consideration of a related difficulty. He writes, "[A] problem remained to trouble me. . . . I had no clear and explicit grasp of the cause of evil."[66] Importantly, Augustine reiterates his earlier-stated belief about God: "[W]hatever you are, you are incorruptible."[67] The openness of his phrasing here is a further reminder that he is not traversing the kind of straight path one finds with a full-fledged argument. However, argument is certainly not absent in Book VII; as he makes the case for God's incorruptibility, Quinn observes, he employs the Aristotelian syllogism.[68]

Eventually, Augustine identifies the source of the problem that troubled him: "I searched for the origin of evil, but I searched in a flawed way and did not see the flaw in my very search."[69] The form of the search itself is flawed, which indicates the need for a transformation. A feature of the *Confessions* and the works to be considered in ensuing chapters is the presentation of opposing methods, wherein a full grasp of the inadequacy of the first opens up the possibility of a new world view. Still trapped in a materialist mind-set, Augustine tries to reconcile God as a kind of stuff that permeates the world with evil as a kind of stuff that somehow exists within the same world.[70] He even considers whether God might have used a material to create the universe that was already tainted by evil.[71] Augustine then launches into a lengthy discussion of astrology, which also offers "no solution."[72] One sees here the way in which autobiography allows Augustine to reveal intellectual humility. Eventually, Augustine pinpoints the flaw in his

65. Starnes, *Augustine's Conversion*, 172.

66. Augustine, *Confessions*, 7.3.4.

67. Augustine, *Confessions*, 7.4.6.

68. Quinn, *Companion to the "Confessions,"* 408n17.

69. Augustine, *Confessions*, 7.5.7.

70. Quinn, *Companion to the "Confessions,"* 351.

71. Augustine, *Confessions*, 7.5.7.

72. Augustine, *Confessions*, 7.7.11.

search: "I was . . . in externals."[73] In other words, he was exclusively looking outside of himself for answers.[74] Since the roadblock was not where he was looking but how he was looking, some kind of conversion was imminent.

Augustine goes on to relay that he came into contact with "some books of the Platonists."[75] According to Starnes, the books would have been Neoplatonic works, written either by "Plotinus himself or of one or another of his disciples, imitators or translators."[76] Before tackling how these Neoplatonic works impacted Augustine, an aside regarding Plato himself is necessary. Paul S. MacDonald holds that a form of conversion distinct from religious conversion emerged in Plato's time. He points to a passage in Plato's *Republic*, written around 375 BC,[77] as an example of this new form of conversion. The passage refers to a "conversion of the soul," as well as "an art of bringing this about."[78] In such a conversion, a person is "turned around from the world of becoming . . . to endure the contemplation of essence and the brightest region of being."[79] MacDonald asserts that Augustine would have been "well aware" of this passage and its conversional dimension.[80]

The impact of Neoplatonic works, in particular, is described by Augustine this way: "I was admonished to return into myself."[81] Here, in chapter 10, lies Augustine's commencement of a new approach—one that does not contain the "flaw" he referred to earlier. The fruit of this new approach is reproduced below:

---

73. Augustine, *Confessions*, 7.7.11.

74. Starnes, *Augustine's Conversion*, 177.

75. Augustine, *Confessions*, 7.9.13.

76. Starnes, *Augustine's Conversion*, 182. See also Quinn, *Companion to the "Confessions,"* 411n30.

77. Pappas, *Guidebook to Plato and the "Republic,"* 11.

78. Plato, *Republic*, 135 [518d].

79. Plato, *Republic*, 135 [518c]. MacDonald refers to this passage in "Philosophical Conversion," 306–7.

80. MacDonald, "Philosophical Conversion," 306.

81. Augustine, *Confessions*, 7.10.16.

With you as my guide I entered into my innermost cita-
del, and was given power to do so because you had become my helper. I entered and with my soul's eye, such as
it was, saw above that same eye of my soul the immutable
light higher than my mind—not the light of every day,
obvious to anyone. . . . It [namely, the immutable light]
transcended my mind, not in the way that oil floats on
water, nor as heaven is above earth. It was superior because it made me, and I was inferior because I was made
by it. The person who knows the truth knows it, and he
who knows it knows eternity.[82]

Several points must be made about this passage. The first point
is that the passage is not entirely unique in Book VII; a similar
ascent is described in chapter 17. The question naturally arises
as to whether these are two different ascents or two accounts of
the same ascent. About this question, Stephen Menn remarks,
"[T]here is no hope, and no point, of deciding."[83] This should not
dismay us since, as Menn goes on to say, "There is no chronologi-
cal development among the . . . ascent passages."[84] While affirming
Menn's statements, this book will treat the passage above as ex-
pressing the effect of conversion, and it will treat what is described
in chapter 17 as conversion proper. One reason for this approach
is that this book portrays conversion as definitive, hence it pri-
oritizes that which does not have intervening reflection.[85] Another

82. Augustine, *Confessions*, 7.10.16. Phillip Cary notes that in this passage,
Augustine "[stresses] not only the difference between the intelligible light and
sensible light (the familiar Platonist contrast between the vision of the mind's
eye and the vision of the eye of the body), but also the difference between the
mind's eye and the divine light it sees." Cary, *Augustine's Invention of the Inner
Self*, 39.

83. Menn, *Descartes and Augustine*, 140n10.

84. Menn, *Descartes and Augustine*, 140n10.

85. In Book IX, during a conversation about God with Monica at Ostia,
Augustine claims he and she had a vision. Menn asserts that it is "hopeless
to look for development between [what is described in chapters 10 and 17 of
Book VII] and the 'vision of Ostia.'" Menn, *Descartes and Augustine*, 140n10.
What is described in chapter 17 remains the best candidate for the label of
conversion proper since it stands in Book VII, which has intellectual transformation as its theme; Book IX, in contrast, treats Augustine's baptism and the

reason is that this book judges Book VII to induce conversion in the reader, so the textual location that is not followed by further enticement, namely, chapter 17, merits priority.

The second point to make is that the passage above involves a new conception of mind and a new conception of God, both of which are available to the reader. Menn parses the process this way: "the soul withdraws from the contemplation of bodies and [enters] into itself, so that it can perceive itself in the proper manner . . . ; then it ascends to contemplate God."[86] The presence of the term "higher" in the passage is vital inasmuch as it powers this process. As Starnes avers, Augustine not only "saw . . . the incorporeal reality of his own thinking" but also accepted that "[h]is thought itself could not be [an] immutable principle because . . . like all else in creation, [it] was mutable."[87] Another aspect of Augustine's new conception of mind is tied directly to the abandonment of materialism. As Menn explains,

> When [Augustine] believed that God was corporeal, he could not conceive him as a nature different from the mind, except as the whole is different from the part; now he has perceived God as incorporeal by conceiving him as the immutable standard by which the mutable mind judges and is judged. The relation between God and the mind remains intimate, but it is a relation of a type found in incorporeal things, not the relation of whole to part.[88]

One can see embedded in this development the prospect of a solution to Augustine's problem regarding evil. The mind is separate from, yet free to choose to work with, an immutable standard. Augustine has more to say, however, before he returns to the problem that got him here.

---

death of Monica. For further analysis of the vision of Ostia, see Dupont and Stróżyński, "Augustine's Ostia Revisited."

86. Menn, *Descartes and Augustine*, 141. It should be acknowledged that Menn does not judge the *Confessions*, in particular, to offer enough detail for the reader to reproduce the ascent. See Menn, *Descartes and Augustine*, 148.

87. Starnes, *Augustine's Conversion*, 184.

88. Menn, *Descartes and Augustine*, 140.

The third point regards the environment in which the soul may perceive itself properly. To obtain a vision of the immutable light, Anthony Kenney writes, "[Augustine] withdraws into the self, . . . ignoring the senses and attendant distractions."[89] Distractions would surely include family, friends, neighbors, and so forth. That being alone was a condition for Augustine's ascent heightens the import of privately engaging Book VII.

The fourth and final point is that, as Starnes states, "a vision [of the immutable light] . . . is in principle available to all mankind."[90] Put differently, such a vision is, in principle, available to both Christians and non-Christians. Recall that Augustine himself had not been baptized when his vision occurred in 386,[91] nor had he read the Bible in a serious manner.[92] Readers can be led to think otherwise by the splendor of his description. But as Starnes states, this was "not . . . a private vision he attained through some special revelation in such a way that he was unable to explain the road which led him to it."[93] That Augustine could and did detail that road, and that the road is available for others to travel via cognitive imitation, places the event outside the category of religious conversion.[94]

Coupled with the breakthrough of the vision of chapter 10 is a warning to the reader about the airiness of merely holding a correct conception of God.[95] It was "[t]hrough a man puffed up with monstrous pride"[96] that Augustine came into contact with the books of the Platonists; the statement itself serves as a caution about the value of what one gathers from such books. Recall that the *Confessions* is written from the standpoint of having not

89. Kenney, *Contemplation and Classical Christianity*, 66.

90. Starnes, *Augustine's Conversion*, 182.

91. Quinn, *Companion to the "Confessions"*, 415n59.

92. Augustine, *Confessions*, 7.20.26.

93. Starnes, *Augustine's Conversion*, 186.

94. The contrasting view of Peter King should be acknowledged here. He labels Augustine's particular form of ascent "a thoroughly Christian enterprise." King, "Augustine's Anti-Platonist Ascents," 25.

95. Starnes, *Augustine's Conversion*, 183.

96. Augustine, *Confessions*, 7.9.13.

only a correct conception of God but a full relationship with God. Now, consider Aristotle's conception of God. As Adam Drozdek observes, "The Unmoved Mover is a footnote in Aristotle's system, limited to passively performing one role: to exist so that it can be a final cause—and nothing else."[97] The reason why Augustine's vision of the immutable light nevertheless marks a transformation relates to his personal story; completely abandoning materialism means completely abandoning Manichaeism, which in turn opens the door for Christianity and the Bible to be given a fresh consideration. This context influences the tone of statements that come after the vision of chapter 10, such as: "That which truly is is that which unchangeably abides."[98] Knowing that the goal is allegiance to that which truly is, not solely knowledge of that which truly is, widens the statement's implications.

Augustine finally returns to the problem that appeared to sidetrack him but ultimately facilitated his—and potentially the reader's—vision: the problem of the origin of evil. Now that the immutable light is his standard, he can solve the problem. He writes,

> [T]he evil into whose origins I was inquiring is not a substance, for if it were a substance, it would be good. Either it would be an incorruptible substance, a great good indeed, or a corruptible substance, which could be corrupted only if it were good. . . . You made all things good, and there are absolutely no substances which you did not make. . . . For you evil does not exist at all.[99]

It is plain how far Augustine has come, from wondering whether God had used a kind of corrupt substance to create the universe to seeing evil as neither a substance nor something God has any causal connection to. As Starnes sums it up, "[Evil] could only exist for . . . intelligent creatures who can both know the absolute good (God) and will some lesser (created) good."[100] Having given con-

---

97. Drozdek, *Greek Philosophers as Theologians*, 183.

98. Augustine, *Confessions*, 7.11.17.

99. Augustine, *Confessions*, 7.12.18–7.13.19.

100. Starnes, *Augustine's Conversion*, 187. Parentheses in the original.

sideration to a view that essentially blames God for evil, Augustine now turns the critical lens towards himself and his mind. In this new model, as Menn explains, "the soul turns away from God of its own free choice, and retains the ability to return if it can rise above the senses and the passions of the body."[101] To accurately know that one is turning away from God requires, of course, a correct conception of God. Making precisely this point, Augustine writes, "[I] saw you to be infinite in another sense, and this way of seeing you did not come from the flesh."[102] Quinn describes this new way of seeing succinctly: "His seeing was intellectual"—"[it] was the outcome of analysis."[103]

With so much emphasis on a new, intellectual way of seeing, the reader might be tempted to question whether seeing with the eye of the body has any value. In chapter 15, Augustine addresses the matter. He writes,

> I turned my gaze on [worldly] things. I saw that to you they owe their existence, and that in you all things are finite, not in the sense that the space they occupy is bounded but in the sense that you hold all things in your hand by your truth. So all things are real insofar as they have being, and the term 'falsehood' applies only when something is thought to have being which does not.[104]

No longer bound to materialism, Augustine can ascertain, as Menn explains, "that things are contained in God because God is the Truth comprehending the forms of the things. The things exist only because they receive form, thus only because they are 'contained' in God, without being a part of God or having a part of him in them."[105] The advance Augustine has made here is striking because of its contrast with where he stood at the outset of

---

101. Menn, *Descartes and Augustine*, 141.

102. Augustine, *Confessions*, 7.14.20.

103. Quinn, *Companion to the "Confessions,"* 367 and 421n81.

104. Augustine, *Confessions*, 7.15.21.

105. Menn, *Descartes and Augustine*, 173. Frederick Ginascol remarks that the Neoplatonic Augustinianism that grew out of Augustine's writings "constantly verged upon the denial of the real existence of nature." Ginascol, "The Question of Universals," 325.

Book VII. Far from seeing matter as eternal, he now judges that matter could not even be said to exist were it not for God holding it—a metaphor, to be sure, since Augustine commenced Book VII by stating that God is not "in the shape of the human body." While the metaphor is simple, the point Augustine is making is both complex and, to contemporary sensibilities, peculiar. As Vaught explains the passage, "[T]ruth is equated with being, where to be and to be true are the same, and where to be true is to be a product of God's creative act."[106]

The abstract discussion that Augustine has entered into as a result of the vision of chapter 10 comes to a halt in chapter 17 with a return to explicit autobiography. He writes,

> I was not stable in the enjoyment of my God. I was caught up to you by your beauty and quickly torn away from you by my weight. With a groan I crashed into inferior things. This weight was my sexual habit. But with me there remained a memory of you.[107]

Two points must be made about this passage. First, Augustine already warned that knowledge of God gained through intellectual vision has a kind of airiness; now, thanks to the form of autobiography, he shares a personal reason as to why a correct concept of God without allegiance to God can be hollow. Importantly, Augustine will shortly speak of "ruts of habit"[108] as inhibiting his vision of the light, thus broadening the category so that the reader may contemplate his or her own blockades. Second, a clarification is necessary regarding Augustine's statement about memory of God. For Augustine, God is "in the memory only from the time in which he is consciously apprehended,"[109] as Gerard O'Daly states. Therefore, the memory is not a kind of Platonic recollection. One might rightfully ask if the memory in question is that gained from learning of God through Monica in childhood, but the context of the statement makes this unlikely. Instead, as Vaught asserts,

---

106. Vaught, *Encounters with God*, 48.
107. Augustine, *Confessions*, 7.17.23.
108. Augustine, *Confessions*, 7.17.23.
109. O'Daly, *Augustine's Philosophy of Mind*, 212.

"it seems reasonable to believe that the memory to which Augustine is referring is a recollection of the experience he has just been recounting."[110]

Next, Augustine once more describes his ascent to God—and this ascent may appropriately be labeled the moment of conversion. He writes,

> [S]tep by step I ascended from bodies to the soul which perceives through the body, and from there to its inward force, to which bodily senses report external sensations, this being as high as the beasts go. From there again I ascended to the power of reasoning to which is to be attributed the power of judging the deliverances of the bodily senses. This power, which in myself I found to be mutable, raised itself to the level of its own intelligence, and led my thinking out of the ruts of habit. It withdrew itself from the contradictory swarms of imaginative fantasies, so as to discover the light by which it was flooded. . . . [I]n the flash of a trembling glance [my mind] attained to that which is. At that moment I saw your "invisible nature understood through the things which are made" (Rom. 1: 20).[111]

Similar to his analysis of chapter 10, Quinn describes this ascent as "a self-wrought intuition of pure existence, not a mystical benison to which he passively raised."[112] But the active aspect of the vision—or glance—is more pronounced here. Augustine "moves gradually through a series of levels from the finite to the infinite," as Vaught observes.[113] Several aspects of the passage firmly legitimate the invocation of the term conversion as opposed to religious conversion: he describes the ascent as gradual; the ascent begins with the mundane, namely, bodies; he states "I ascended" and employs the pronoun amply; and he relays that his power of judging "raised itself" and "withdrew itself." All of these elements render the ascent available to the reader via cognitive imitation.

110. Vaught, *Encounters with God*, 50.
111. Augustine, *Confessions*, 7.17.23.
112. Quinn, *Companion to the "Confessions,"* 391.
113. Vaught, *Encounters with God*, 52.

Next, Augustine once again loses his clasp on God: "I did not possess the strength to keep my vision fixed. My weakness reasserted itself, and I returned to my customary condition."[114] Even if Augustine could keep his vision fixed, it would not be for long; as Vaught states, "[t]he philosopher only sees God momentarily."[115] Therefore, in chapter 18, Augustine will voice that he needs a mediator between himself and God. This should not be taken, however, as downplaying the significance of the conversion. Augustine has not merely ceased subscription to materialism—he has definitively abandoned materialism. Potentially, the reader has as well.

Even after "learning from [the books of the Platonists] to seek for immaterial truth,"[116] as Augustine himself puts it, he is still unable to understand how God could become flesh in the person of Jesus Christ.[117] This prompts him to turn to the books of Scripture. After doing so, he realizes that "he must move from a philosophical to a Christian transformation," as Vaught asserts.[118] The reader learns about that transformation in Book VIII and, in a smaller measure, in Book IX.[119] In Book X, Augustine ceases autobiography and commences an explanation of life from a cosmic standpoint. In short, Augustine starts over. Cognitive imitation has been replaced by argumentation—and private engagement, one would imagine, has shifted from expectation to suggestion. Readers who have abandoned materialism via Book VII and fully accept the implications of that abandonment can start over with Augustine.

---

114. Augustine, *Confessions*, 7.17.23.

115. Vaught, *Encounters with God*, 53.

116. Augustine, *Confessions*, 7.20.26.

117. Vaught, *Encounters with God*, 61.

118. Vaught, *Encounters with God*, 61.

119. It should be noted that in Book VIII, Augustine's conception of himself becomes, with God's help, even clearer. This time, the clarification is moral, rather than intellectual, in nature. He writes, "[Y]ou thrust me before my own eyes so that I should discover my iniquity and hate it." Augustine, *Confessions*, 8.7.16.

2

Conversion in the First and Second Meditation in René Descartes's *Meditations*

Background

RENÉ DESCARTES WAS BORN on March 31, 1596 in the town of La Haye (present-day Descartes, France). The town's name was changed to Descartes in 1967 to honor him. Several members of his extended family were the recipients of royal appointments, including his own father, Joachim, who worked at an appeals court.[1] Put sparsely, Descartes had an upper-class upbringing; yet this did not yield a childhood that was problem-free and without tragedy. Descartes's mother, Jeanne, took primary responsibility for raising him and his siblings since Joachim was required to live near the court for several months a year—and the court was more than 100 miles away.[2] Then, tragically, just days after giving birth to and losing her fifth child in 1597, Jeanne herself died. Descartes would now be raised by his maternal grandmother, Jeanne Sain, and his

1. Clarke, *Descartes*, 9.
2. Clarke, *Descartes*, 9.

nurse.[3] Furthermore, Joachim's absence, already felt by the family, was increased to six months in 1600.[4]

It was probably in 1607 that Descartes left home for Collège Royal Henry-Le-Grand, a Jesuit school in La Flèche, France.[5] His brother, Pierre, was already a boarder at the school.[6] Descartes's studies there involved two stages. The first stage included grammar, rhetoric, and classics, as well as how to write in Latin and Greek;[7] the second included logic, mathematics, physics, and metaphysics.[8] When looking at the subjects, one's eyes are drawn to logic and metaphysics as potential sources of influence on Descartes; this is only the case in a negative sense. The adult Descartes opposed, for example, the idea of logic as providing "an account of scientific demonstration" and "a set of rules for thinking correctly," two things Stephen Gaukroger claims were present in the textbooks at the Collège.[9] For a positive early influence, one must instead look to mathematics. For example, as Edwin Curley relays, "[T]he teachers used the texts of the Jesuit mathematician Christopher Clavius, who argued that mathematics was superior to the other supposed sciences . . . because it succeeded in eliminating all doubt."[10] Esteem for mathematics, especially its ability to remove doubt and to be airtight in its succeeding steps, undergirds the adult Descartes's philosophy.

Another lasting philosophical influence from the Collège—one even more surprising than mathematics—is the practice of spiritual retreats. Each year the students went on a short retreat based on the *Spiritual Exercises* of Ignatius of Loyola, the founder of the Jesuit religious order.[11] Although there is no direct evidence

3. Clarke, *Descartes*, 10.

4. Clarke, *Descartes*, 9.

5. Clarke, *Descartes*, 24.

6. Clarke, *Descartes*, 24.

7. Clarke, *Descartes*, 17.

8. Clarke, *Descartes*, 19.

9. Gaukroger, *Descartes*, 54.

10. Curley, "Descartes," 721.

11. Clarke, *Descartes*, 28.

that Descartes participated in the retreats, Zeno Vendler judges that he "most likely" did—and even if he did not, he would have heard about them from instructors and classmates.[12] The way in which the retreats, or knowledge of the retreats, shaped Descartes's philosophy will be unpacked in due course.

Descartes completed his studies at the Collège, likely in 1615.[13] He then attended the University of Poitiers, earning a bachelor's degree and a law degree.[14] Next, he enlisted in the army in Breda, the United Provinces (present-day Netherlands).[15] There he met Isaac Beeckman, a medical doctor several years older who had come to Breda in 1618 to visit his girlfriend.[16] Descartes befriended Beeckman, whose scientific and mathematical knowledge impressed and inspired him.[17]

The winter of 1619 stands out when reviewing Descartes's past. In his *Discourse on the Method of Rightly Conducting One's Reason and of Seeking Truth in the Sciences*, published almost two decades later, he recollects:

> [T]he onset of winter detained me in quarters where, finding no conversation to divert me and fortunately no cares or passions to trouble me, I stayed all day shut up alone in a stove-heated room, where I was completely free to converse with myself about my own thoughts.[18]

A set of substantial events occurred in this environment on November 10.[19] Anthony Kenny summarizes them as follows:

12. Vendler, "Descartes' Exercises," 194.

13. Clarke, *Descartes*, 32.

14. Clarke, *Descartes*, 32.

15. Clarke, *Descartes*, 42.

16. Clarke, *Descartes*, 42.

17. Clarke, *Descartes*, 42.

18. Descartes, *Discourse on the Method*, 1:116 [VI 11]. The internal reference, namely, the Adam-Tannery reference, is given in square brackets.

19. The events are described in biographer Adrien Baillet's *Vie de Monsieur Descartes*, published in 1691. Baillet utilizes Descartes's *Olympica*, "a twelve-page manuscript which was never published and has since been lost." See Keevak, "Descartes's Dreams," 373.

> He conceived the idea of undertaking, single-handed,
> a reform of human learning that would display all dis-
> ciplines as branches of a single wonderful science. His
> conviction of vocation was reinforced when, that night,
> he had three dreams that he regarded as prophetic.[20]

The content of the dreams is complicated and has received extensive interpretation; those details need not be tackled here. What
is pertinent is that, according to Gaukroger, he acted on the vocation: he began writing *Rules for the Direction of the Mind*.[21] In
this treatise, explains Gary Hatfield, "[Descartes] sought to extend
a method like that in mathematics to 'any subject whatsoever.'"[22]
The treatise was abandoned around 1628;[23] however, it was published posthumously in an incomplete form. Descartes would later
compress the method into four rules in a section of the *Discourse*.[24]

The next phase of Descartes's life stands in contrast to being
shut up in a stove-heated room. In the *Discourse*, he recalls being
content with the maxims gained through the vision and dreams
and with his religious beliefs, but the remainder needed to be
reassessed:

> I took the decision that, as far as the rest of my opinions
> were concerned, I could freely undertake to rid myself
> of them. And seeing that I expected to be better able
> to complete this task in the company of others than by
> remaining shut any longer in the stove-heated room
> in which I had had all these thoughts, I set out on my
> travels again before winter was over. And through all the
> next nine years I did nothing but wander through the
> world.[25]

---

20. Kenny, *Rise of Modern Philosophy*, 34.

21. Gaukroger, *Descartes*, 111.

22. Hatfield, *Routledge Guidebook*, 15. The quoted material is from Descartes, *Rules*, 1:17 [X 374].

23. Gaukroger, *Descartes*, 111.

24. Hatfield, *Routledge Guidebook*, 16. For the rules, see Descartes, *Discourse on the Method*, 1:120 [VI 18–19].

25. Descartes, *Discourse on the Method*, 1:125 [VI 28].

Some of this travel was outside of France, and being exposed to other cultures brought about the reassessing of beliefs that he sought.[26] Amidst his travels, Descartes began corresponding with Marin Mersenne, an influential mathematician, philosopher, and scientist from France. In late 1628 Descartes would return to the United Provinces and remain there, as Hatfield notes, for more than twenty years.[27]

In 1629 Descartes moved into a castle in the city of Franeker, where, as Desmond Clarke notes, "he enjoyed . . . the privacy that he claimed to need for his studies."[28] Descartes claims it was here that he made his first "meditations."[29] After six months, he left the castle and began moving to different residences in the United Provinces. At each one, he endeavored to keep his address a secret from others—something that further served his need for privacy while studying.[30]

Hatfield points to a letter by Descartes in 1630 as confirming a change in outlook during this period. In the letter, Descartes claims to have discovered "'how to demonstrate metaphysical truths in a manner which is more evident than the demonstrations of geometry.'"[31] This statement contrasts with Descartes's earlier view of mathematics as "the ultimate standard of certainty," as Hatfield puts it.[32]

In 1637 Descartes published the aforementioned *Discourse*, which he wrote in French. As already hinted at, this work features both autobiography and philosophy. In the middle of the work, Descartes makes his most famous statement: "Je pense, donc je suis." A widespread English translation of the statement reads,

---

26. Clarke, *Descartes*, 63.

27. Hatfield, *Routledge Guidebook*, 18.

28. Clarke, *Descartes*, 98.

29. Descartes, *Discourse on Method*, 1:126 [VI 31]. While there, he wrote a treatise that would develop into the *Meditations*. Clarke, *Descartes*, 101.

30. Clarke, *Descartes*, 97.

31. Hatfield, *Routledge Guidebook*, 19.

32. Hatfield, *Routledge Guidebook*, 19.

"I think, therefore I am"; however, "I am thinking, therefore I exist" is a more accurate translation.[33]

Descartes began writing the *Meditations* in 1639, completed a preliminary version in 1640, and published the work in 1641.[34] The full title of the work is *Meditations on First Philosophy, in Which the Existence of God and the Immortality of the Soul Are Demonstrated.*[35] It was written in Latin, which was "the normal language for instruction at universities," thus the work would be "accessible to academic readers all over Europe."[36] In fact, as Kurt Smith states, the *Meditations* was "[t]he first 'textbook' that Descartes explicitly intended to be used by professors in the classroom."[37] Included in the first edition were objections and replies, as Descartes had circulated the manuscript to others for reaction before publication. A French translation of the *Meditations*, carried out by Louis-Charles d'Albert and approved by Descartes, was published in 1647.

As announced at the outset of this book, Descartes's post-*Meditations* life will not be reviewed in detail. It can simply be pointed out that Descartes continued to write. In 1644, for example, he published *Principles of Philosophy*, a work that he "hoped . . . would replace the prevailing Aristotelian curriculum in colleges and universities, at least in metaphysics and physics," as Hatfield relays.[38] Descartes died of pneumonia in Stockholm on February 11, 1650.[39]

33. Descartes, *Discourse on the Method*, 1:127 [VI 32]. Italics removed.

34. Gaukroger, *Descartes*, xvii.

35. Stephen Menn points out that when one says the initial four words of the title, one should put emphasis on the word "first." Menn, *Descartes and Augustine*, 52n34.

36. Clarke, *Descartes*, 144.

37. Smith, *Descartes Dictionary*, 24.

38. Hatfield, *Routledge Guidebook*, 30.

39. Gaukroger, *Descartes*, 417.

The *Meditations* as a Conversion Work

To label the *Meditations* as containing and inducing conversion is uncontroversial. As Harry Frankfurt asserts, "Descartes's aim is to guide the reader to intellectual salvation by recounting his own discovery of reason and his escape thereby from the benighted reliance on his senses."[40] Frankfurt's use of "salvation" anticipates the related term, conversion, which he indeed goes on to invoke:

> [T]he First Meditation . . . [wrecks] the thoughtless con-
> fidence in sense perception with which common sense
> is generally content. It is intended to render the philo-
> sophical novice to whom Descartes addresses himself,
> and in whose behalf he speaks, susceptible to an intel-
> lectual conversion.[41]

Containing six meditations in total, one can gather from Frankfurt's phrasing that conversion occurs closer to the beginning of the *Meditations* than the end—and it does. Recall that in this book, conversion means abandoning a world view and starting over.[42] In the *Meditations*, the abandonment occurs in the Second Meditation and the starting over occurs in the Third. As Hatfield explains, "Once the meditator becomes accustomed to clear and distinct intellectual perception, metaphysical conclusions fall fast and thick in Meditations 3–6."[43] A point of contrast arises here between Augustine's *Confessions* and Descartes's *Meditations*. Even though both works are autobiographical in character and written in the first person, Books I to VI of the *Confessions* offer an extensive personal background and a lengthy build-up to starting over, whereas the First Meditation offers almost no background. Moreover, whereas the arc of conversion in Book VII of the *Confessions* spans years, it spans days in the *Meditations*.

---

40. Frankfurt, *Demons, Dreamers, and Madmen*, 5.

41. Frankfurt, *Demons, Dreamers, and Madmen*, 19–20.

42. This definition is adapted from MacDonald, "Philosophical Conversion," 304.

43. Hatfield, *Routledge Guidebook*, 66.

The absence of biographical detail at the outset of the *Meditations* signals that instructional—not autobiographical—concerns take precedence. The most basic sense in which they dominate is that Descartes did not spend six days in a room recording his thoughts.[44] And yet, as the peculiarity and specificity of six days suggests, they are not purely a fabrication. It was mentioned earlier that there is a link between the retreats at the Collège in La Flèche and the *Meditations*. Just like the retreats at the Collège, *Meditations* spans six days.[45] L. J. Beck deems this beyond coincidence.[46] Such a judgment is aided by additional similarities between the retreats and the *Meditations*, which will be discussed in detail shortly. So, while the six days are indeed a literary device, they have biographical roots. A further sense in which the six Meditations are rooted in history is found in the aforementioned fact that Descartes did conduct "meditations" while staying at the castle in Franeker in 1629. Further still, in the Preface to the Reader he states, "[I]n the *Meditations*, I will set out the very thoughts which have enabled me . . . to arrive at a certain and evident knowledge of the truth."[47] In alignment with this statement, Frankfurt asserts, "[T]he First Meditation represents an early stage of his own philosophical thinking."[48] Similar to Augustine at the outset of Book VII of the *Confessions*, Descartes readopts an undeveloped viewpoint from his past—specifically, that of unsophisticated empiricism.[49] His presentation of the viewpoint is, as noted above, shaped by instructional concerns and placed in a fictional setting. Therefore, just as with Augustine in the *Confessions*, the "I" of the *Meditations*

44. Hatfield, *Routledge Guidebook*, 52.

45. For a list of statements made in the *Meditations* that show the days to be successive, see Vendler, "Descartes' Exercises," 201. It should be noted that the retreats took place during Holy Week and spanned eight days; however, excluding the two Sundays brings the number to six.

46. Beck, *Metaphysics of Descartes*, 32.

47. Descartes, *Meditations*, 2:8 [VII 10]. Referred to in Hatfield, *Routledge Guidebook*, 52.

48. Frankfurt, *Demons, Dreamers, and Madmen*, 5. For a contrasting view, see Broughton, *Descartes's Method of Doubt*, 23.

49. See Frankfurt, *Demons, Dreamers, and Madmen*, 84–86.

should be labeled Descartes the narrator. Another similarity between the works lies in Robert McMahon's observation that the
reader of the *Confessions* "impersonates the narrator's 'I' in his
dialogue with God"—he or she "necessarily becomes Augustine
the narrator."[50] This applies to the *Meditations* as well, with the
caveat that readers who do not have a "thoughtless confidence in
sense perception," to repeat Frankfurt's words, experience the First
Meditation's scrutiny of the senses as a reinforcement rather than
an exercise. For Descartes, however, such readers are few and far
between. This raises a question about the profile of those in whom
the *Meditations* seeks to induce conversion.

If one limits oneself to the front matter, the *Meditations* is said
to be aimed towards "unbelievers," or more specifically, persons
who will not adopt a religion until the existence of God and the
immortality of the soul "are proved to them by natural reason."[51]
Descartes goes on to describe the *Meditations* as bolstering a declaration of the Fifth Lateran Council, which was held from 1512 to
1517. The declaration laments the appearance of "errors . . . concerning the nature of the rational soul, namely, that it is mortal, or
one in all men"—and it laments, "[S]ome . . . affirmed that this is
true at least according to philosophy."[52]

If one goes outside of the front matter, the *Meditations* are
shown to have a different target audience. Noteworthy is a personal
letter from Descartes to Mersenne in 1641 that requests confiden-
tiality. In the letter, Descartes states that in the *Meditations* he puts
forth "the foundations of [his] physics."[53] He then writes, "[P]lease
do not tell people, for that might make it harder for supporters
of Aristotle to approve [the foundations]."[54] And finally, disclosing
one reason for tailoring the work like a retreat instead of a strict

---

50. McMahon, *Medieval Meditative Ascent*, 92.

51. Descartes, *Meditations*, 2:3 [VII 2]. Clarke highlights something that
perplexed a great many, including Mersenne: "there is not a word about the
'immortality' of the soul in the *Meditations.*" Clarke, *Descartes*, 457n87.

52. Fifth Lateran Council, "The Human Soul," 237 [*Denzinger-Bannwart*
738; *Denzinger-Schönmetzer* 1440].

53. Descartes, "To Mersenne, 8 January 1641," 3:173 [III 298].

54. Descartes, "To Mersenne, 8 January 1641," 3:173 [III 298].

argument, he writes, "I hope that readers will gradually get used to my principles, and recognize their truth, before they notice that they destroy the principles of Aristotle."[55] The assumption embedded in his statement is accurate: the work does challenge the then-dominant outlook of Aristotle. It is worth reproducing Hatfield's comments on the matter in full:

> At the core of the Aristotelian conception of the knower lay a sense-based epistemology, which was distilled into the slogan, "Nothing is in the intellect that was not first in the senses." As elaborated by Thomas Aquinas and subsequent scholastic Aristotelians, this implied that all knowledge, including knowledge of God, the soul, and the truths of mathematics, is attained by the intellectual abstraction of universals from sensory particulars. In the course of the *Meditations*, Descartes reaches the opposite conclusion, that the things known first and known best are not known by or through the senses, but through the independent operation of the intellect. Descartes's replacement dictum might be phrased, "Nothing is accepted from the senses, that was not first in the intellect."[56]

Alongside intercepting an academic viewpoint likely held by many of his potential readers, Descartes was intercepting an attitude that many carry over from childhood. As Hatfield explains, for Descartes, our childhood habit is to presume that sensations give us immediate knowledge of the properties of objects and that objects give us pictures of themselves.[57] The dawning of adulthood does not mean this attitude fades away. "[I]n Descartes's view," writes Hatfield, "the untutored individual [is] likely to be nearly wholly immersed in the senses."[58] In challenging a theory of knowledge widespread consciously in the academy and unconsciously in the general population, Descartes judged meditation to be a prudent means of opposition. The personal nature of the meditation made it conducive to eliciting the abandonment of a deep-seated

---

55. Descartes, "To Mersenne, 8 January 1641," 3:173 [III 298].

56. Hatfield, "Descartes's *Meditations*," 50–51.

57. Hatfield, "Descartes's *Meditations*," 51.

58. Hatfield, "Descartes's *Meditations*," 42.

outlook. As Hatfield relays, Descartes "invites each individual to establish the merits of the proposed truths for him- or herself."[59] The remaining task of this section is to identify the specific moment of conversion. As noted in the Introduction of this book, the *Meditations* is unique in that there is separation between the containment and induction of conversion. The separation is slight, as both occur in the Second Meditation and only a few paragraphs apart. Conversion is contained in Descartes's announcement, "At last I have discovered it—thought; this alone is inseparable from me."[60] It should be noted that this announcement has a different meaning[61] and a different approach to imitation[62] than the famous statement, "I am thinking, therefore I exist," found in the *Discourse*.[63] With respect to the induction of conversion, one finds it shortly after in a thought experiment involving wax from a honeycomb.[64]

Cognitive Imitation

The spectre of cognitive imitation is raised by Descartes in the Preface to the Reader: "I would not urge anyone to read this book except those who are able and willing to meditate seriously with me."[65] Descartes chose the word meditation over the more usual

---

59. Hatfield, *Routledge Guidebook*, 43.

60. Descartes, *Meditations*, 2:18 [27].

61. Broughton, *Descartes's Method of Doubt*, 110; Frankfurt, *Demons, Dreamers, and Madmen*, 138.

62. In the *Discourse*, "[Descartes] positively discourages people at large to follow him," as Vendler relays. Vendler, "Descartes' Exercises," 199. See Descartes, *Discourse on the Method*, 1:118 [VI 15].

63. To be precise, a modified form of the famous statement does appear in a reply to an objection in the *Meditations*. See Descartes, *Meditations*, 2:100 [VII 140].

64. Descartes, *Meditations*, 2:21 [VII 31].

65. Descartes, *Meditations*, 2:6 [VII 9]. Part of the reason for the requirement of meditating "seriously" is captured in a remark by Hatfield: "For an inattentive or lazy reader, [the approach of the *Meditations*] would not compel assent, for it did not offer an unbroken chain of demonstration." Hatfield, *Routledge Guidebook*, 43.

disputation, Beck relays, in order to stress "the special way in which his work should be read and studied."[66] As Beck explains, Descartes wants the reader "to re-think with him his own thoughts," as opposed to the procedure common up to his time, namely, "to examine . . . theses argued out in syllogistic form."[67]

The ways in which the reader is to imitate Descartes come to light through a further consideration of Ignatian influence on the *Meditations*. Reflections by Walter Stohrer, Vendler, and Hatfield are helpful in this effort. Stohrer detects "a specifically Ignatian influence on the content, structure, [and] expression of Descartes's later thought."[68] One form of influence is tied to Ignatius's description of his exercises as "preparing and disposing the soul to rid itself of all inordinate attachments."[69] According to Stohrer, Descartes appropriates this process at the outset of the *Meditations*: "methodic doubt has a distinctly purgative purpose."[70] Another form of influence identified by Stohrer regards "the primary means for achieving greater mental development" in the *Exercises*.[71] Among the means are "uninterrupted thought processes, . . . frequent repetitions of earlier reflective experiences, and careful notation of where and why deeper insight was achieved."[72] Each of these, contends Stohrer, is also found in the *Meditations*. Stohrer's list of means for mental development exudes a cooperative sensitivity.

Vendler contends that just as Ignatius warns of the soul being "inordinately . . . inclined to anything,"[73] Descartes strives to eliminate his "inordinate inclination to trust the senses."[74] The

---

66. Beck, *Metaphysics of Descartes*, 30. See Descartes, *Meditations*, 2:112 [VII 157].

67. Beck, *Metaphysics of Descartes*, 34.

68. Stohrer, "Descartes and Ignatius Loyola," 12. Stohrer acknowledges that Descartes "made no references to the *Exercises* in his works." Stohrer, "Descartes and Ignatius Loyola," 14.

69. Ignatius, *Spiritual Exercises*, §1.

70. Stohrer, "Descartes and Ignatius Loyola," 18.

71. Stohrer, "Descartes and Ignatius Loyola," 26.

72. Stohrer, "Descartes and Ignatius Loyola," 26.

73. Ignatius, *Spiritual Exercises*, §16.

74. Vendler, "Descartes' Exercises," 204.

imitational quality of the *Meditations* is plain here; the reader must attend to and adjust a disposition of him or herself along with Descartes. Eventually, Ignatius carries out an "application of the senses," as he names it, and likewise, Descartes reintroduces the senses in a controlled way in the Second Meditation.[75] Vendler also addresses Descartes's rationale for not referring to the *Exercises* in his writings, despite its influence. If he had described his aim as bringing about "an intellectual 'conversion' in the subject" on par with the spiritual conversion of the *Exercises*, it would have been seen as arrogant, given Ignatius's prominence.[76]

Independent of the consideration of Ignatian influence, Hatfield sheds light on the imitational quality of the *Meditations*. "As readers," writes Hatfield, "we are to place ourselves in the position of the meditator."[77] A person who engages the *Meditations* "must seek to relive the process of doubt and discovery, not merely reading about various cognitive acts but performing them."[78] Hatfield also delves into "striking" parallels between the structure of the *Exercises* and the *Meditations*,[79] including the already mentioned purge that the reader must conduct with Descartes before any illumination can occur,[80] but he adds something new. Hatfield claims that this purging activity also has roots in the Augustinian tradition—and in the *Confessions* itself. This matter must be treated independently as the link between Descartes and Augustine is not as clear-cut as between him and Ignatius.

Catherine Wilson points out that when repeatedly asked about similarities between, for example, an argument in Augustine's *City of God* and in the *Discourse*, Descartes's responses ranged from not being able to obtain Augustine's works in 1638 to accessing the *City of God* at a library and deeming the similarity coincidental in

75. Vendler, "Descartes' Exercises," 207.

76. Vendler, "Descartes' Exercises," 223. This is one of several possible reasons he outlines; see Vendler, "Descartes' Exercises," 220–24.

77. Hatfield, *Routledge Guidebook*, 53.

78. Hatfield, *Routledge Guidebook*, 53.

79. Hatfield, "Descartes's *Meditations*," 44.

80. Hatfield, "Descartes's *Meditations*," 42.

1640.[81] What one should keep in mind when thinking about these responses, contends Wilson, is that Descartes "was not inclined to be generous in acknowledging his intellectual debts."[82] Wilson sees it as probable that Descartes had at least heard lectures on Augustine, but "no one has proved that this is so."[83] Hatfield believes Descartes was "familiar with . . . the Augustinian [tradition] from his contact with [a] Parisian Oratory during the 1620s."[84] It is on this basis that Hatfield sees the *Confessions*, especially Book VII, as a "model" for the *Meditations*; indeed, one finds in both a bracketing of memory and the imagination and a foregrounding of the "mind's eye."[85] As this book seeks to refrain from comparing the works considered in it, the relevance of Hatfield's claim lies in its corroboration of an imitational dynamic in the *Meditations*. In short, one follows, rather than simply agrees with, the narrator of the *Confessions* and the narrator of the *Meditations*.

Private Engagement

At the outset of the *Meditations*, Descartes writes, "I am here quite alone."[86] This condition of solitude is neither accidental nor temporary. Descartes has "arranged . . . a clear stretch of free time" to meditate in this environment.[87] Moreover, he has "expressly rid

81. Wilson, "Descartes and Augustine," 34–35. See also Clarke, *Descartes*, 210; Hatfield, *Routledge Guidebook*, 24; MacDonald, "Philosophical Conversion," 308.

82. Wilson, "Descartes and Augustine," 35.

83. Wilson, "Descartes and Augustine," 40–41.

84. Hatfield, "Descartes's *Meditations*," 43.

85. Hatfield, "Descartes's *Meditations*," 46–47. The term *mind's eye* appears several times in both the *Confessions* and *Meditations*, including in conjunction with repudiating the senses. It should be noted that some scholars reject substantial Ignatian and Augustinian influence on the way that the *Meditations* is written. For a survey of their views, and an argument that one should look instead to Marin Mersenne as influencing the unique style of the *Meditations*, see Hettche, "Descartes and the Augustinian Tradition," 302–6.

86. Descartes, *Meditations*, 2:12 [VII 18].

87. Descartes, *Meditations*, 2:12 [VII 18].

[his] mind of all worries."[88] Once again, one finds here an Ignatian parallel. Stohrer draws attention to the twentieth and final annotation of the *Exercises*.[89] There Ignatius writes,

> Ordinarily, the progress made in the Exercises will be greater, the more the exercitant withdraws from all friends and acquaintances, and from all worldly cares. For example, he can leave the house in which he dwelt and choose another house or room in order to live there in as great privacy as possible, so that he will be free to go to Mass and Vespers every day without any fear that his acquaintances will cause any difficulty.[90]

Stohrer highlights the autobiographical aspect of this, namely, the aforementioned fact that in the winter of 1619, Descartes "stayed all day shut up alone in a stove-heated room," where he was free to "converse with [himself] about [his] own thoughts."[91] In addition, Beck points to a letter from Descartes to Princess Elizabeth in which he expresses the difficulty of searching for truth when not in solitude.[92] For Beck, it is part and parcel of Cartesian method that "[t]he discovery of metaphysical truth is a solitary affair."[93] In light of all of this, and in light of his explicit invitation to the reader to meditate with him, it is plain that he or she ought to read the *Meditations* while alone.

A Map of Conversion in the *Meditations*

Three preliminary notes must be made before commencing the mapping. First, for ease of reading, the mapping will simply refer to Descartes as the person carrying out the meditations, rather than

---

88. Descartes, *Meditations*, 2:12 [VII 18].

89. Stohrer, "Descartes and Ignatius Loyola," 17.

90. Ignatius, *Spiritual Exercises*, §20. Participation in Mass and Vespers are not mentioned by Descartes.

91. Descartes, *Discourse on the Method*, 1:116 [VII 11].

92. Beck, *Metaphysics of Descartes*, 298.

93. Beck, *Metaphysics of Descartes*, 298.

Descartes the narrator.[94] Second, the mapping that follows does not include the objections and replies. The rationale for this must be provided, since in the Preface to the Reader, Descartes states that one should not "pass judgement on the *Meditations*" before reading all of them.[95] The objections and replies, as Hatfield puts it, "stand outside the meditational form of the six Meditations."[96] In the language and context of this book, they stand outside the conversional goal of the first two meditations. As will become clear, the first two meditations seek to illuminate the reader's mind and contain all of the materials for effecting that illumination. In short, it would violate the work's own integrity for a reader to be converted by the replies—or the objections, for that matter. Of course, the scholarly reflections appealed to in the mapping are sometimes informed by them. A third and final preliminary note regards the depth of the mapping. The goal in what follows is to highlight those components of the work that pertain in a preparatory or direct way to the containment and induction of conversion. Thus the general plot points in the arc of conversion are given attention rather than smaller, technical pivots, many of which scholars disagree on.[97]

The First Meditation is entitled "What Can Be Called into Doubt." Descartes reports that "[s]ome years ago" it dawned on him that he accepted many falsehoods during childhood and that he based an "edifice" on those falsehoods in adulthood.[98] Still within the time frame of "some years ago," Descartes relays,

> I realized that it was necessary, once in the course of my life, to demolish everything completely and start again right from the foundations if I wanted to establish anything at all in the sciences that was stable and likely to last.[99]

94. Nor will "the meditator" be used, for this book wants to acknowledge that the *Meditations* contain—as already noted—"the very thoughts" that enabled Descartes to obtain "certain and evident knowledge of the truth."

95. Descartes, *Meditations*, 2:8 [VII 10].

96. Hatfield, *Routledge Guidebook*, 61.

97. See, for example, Wagner, *Squaring the Circle*, 88n38.

98. Descartes, *Meditations*, 2:12 [VII 17].

99. Descartes, *Meditations*, 2:12 [VII 17].

The metaphor invoked here of a building sitting on unstable ground is easily grasped by the reader and naturally involves him or her in the drama underway. Almost as a reflex response, the reader worries if his or her own adult belief system rests on falsehoods accepted during his or her own childhood. Moreover, when Descartes proposes a solution, namely, a demolition, the reader naturally wants to find out more. The casualness with which Descartes proposes the solution also keeps the reader from abandoning the meditation—something possible given the gravity of what Descartes is suggesting.

In the second half of the passage above, Descartes reveals a more personal impetus for the proposed demolition. Hatfield explains that by "the sciences" Descartes means "philosophical disciplines, including metaphysics, natural philosophy, and its branches: mechanics, medicine, and morals."[100] Establishing something "stable and likely to last" in metaphysics is especially important in the *Meditations*. Aristotle referred to metaphysics as first philosophy, and the full title of Descartes's work makes its concern clear: *Meditations on First Philosophy*. To say that these areas are in need of something stable and lasting sounds foreign to contemporary ears, but as Hatfield points out, "[Descartes's] age was a time of intellectual turmoil."[101] What does resonate with readers today is a concern about the verity of one's childhood beliefs. Importantly, the tools for alleviating that concern are provided in the meditations themselves, thus the concern and the means by which it can be alleviated are not bound to Descartes's time. As Frankfurt explains, "[A]t no stage of the work . . . [does] he presume any greater philosophical progress than he himself has led his reader to achieve."[102] Put in the terminology of this book, there is no moment of unreasonably expected cognitive imitation. It follows that even the reader who has only the more general concern of an insecure belief system—and not the specific concern of a basis for "the sciences"—can be rewarded if he or she proceeds.

100. Hatfield, *Routledge Guidebook*, 75.
101. Hatfield, *Routledge Guidebook*, 75.
102. Frankfurt, *Demons, Dreamers, and Madmen*, 8.

Concurrent with Descartes's realization of the need for a demolition is a realization that a mature age is necessary to carry it
out. This is the point on which Descartes pivots into the present.
"[T]oday," he writes, "I have expressly rid my mind of all worries
and arranged for myself a clear stretch of free time. I am here quite
alone, and at last I will devote myself . . . to the general demolition of my opinions."[103] The uniqueness of the *Meditations* as a
philosophical work comes fully into view here, for one would not
expect to be told about the environment in which a manuscript
was penned. As noted earlier, the environment is described so
that the reader can reproduce it. A few sentences later, in making a philosophical point, Descartes provides more detail about
his environment: "I am . . . sitting by [a] fire, wearing a winter
dressing-gown, holding [a] piece of paper in my hands."[104] These
aspects of his environment need not be reproduced by the reader
but they do enhance the sense of joining Descartes in a real-time
philosophical undertaking.

Descartes's next move is to explicate how the demolition will
be carried out. It will not involve trying to show that all of his beliefs are false, he explains, for such a task is impractical. He considers a different approach: "I should . . . hold back my assent from
opinions which are not completely certain and indubitable."[105] This
would still seem to require sifting through all of his beliefs and testing, in some way, for certainty and indubitability. Descartes then
clarifies his approach: "I will go straight for the basic principles on
which all my former beliefs rested."[106] It is not immediately clear
what "basic principles" he has in mind.[107] Since this chapter is interested in mapping conversion, what is relevant here is that "basic
principles" pertain to "criteria or rules . . . used for passing judgment," as Stephen Menn states.[108] In thinking on a criteriological

---

103. Descartes, *Meditations*, 2:12 [VII 18].

104. Descartes, *Meditations*, 2:13 [VII 18].

105. Descartes, *Meditations*, 2:12 [VII 18].

106. Descartes, *Meditations*, 2:12 [VII 18].

107. Wagner, *Squaring the Circle*, 50.

108. Menn, *Descartes and Augustine*, 225.

level, one expects that Descartes's next move will be to tackle how beliefs are acquired in conjunction with the topics of certainty and indubitability. Descartes does precisely that.

Descartes states that the beliefs he has accepted as "most true" are those acquired via the senses. However, the senses can sometimes be wrong, Descartes contends, and "it is prudent never to trust completely those who have deceived us even once."[109] Frankfurt explains that for Descartes, a use of the senses includes hearing someone share a belief—even the belief that God exists.[110] A person who has merely heard that God exists "knows nothing of [the matter] directly."[111] In raising awareness of the presence or absence of directness, to use Frankfurt's term, Descartes is instilling a warning about unwarily assenting. He is also hinting that he will eventually "discover a rule of evidence more reliable than the rules of sensory evidence," as Frankfurt puts it.[112] Importantly, what Descartes is saying here does not contradict his earlier contention that he is sitting by a fire in a winter dressing-gown. The senses have their uses.[113] Trusting the senses completely in the search for foundations is what is problematic. Something stable and lasting in "the sciences," whatever it might be, will have been "purified from all sensory contamination," as Menn puts it.[114]

Descartes turns to other things that we cannot trust completely. Using the example of madmen having delusions that are truthful from their vantage point, he explains that non-madmen

---

109. Descartes, *Meditations*, 2:12 [VII 18].

110. Frankfurt, *Demons, Dreamers, and Madmen*, 44.

111. Frankfurt, *Demons, Dreamers, and Madmen*, 45.

112. Frankfurt, *Demons, Dreamers, and Madmen*, 154.

113. It is worth going beyond the arc of conversion for a moment. As Menn observes, "In the [S]ixth Meditation . . . Descartes restores some cognitive value to sensation. . . . While sensation has no direct theoretical value (does not show us the natures of things), it has a practical value in guiding our use of the body so as to preserve ourselves as a mind-body union; and it has an indirect theoretical value in that we can make some inferences about what the bodies around us must be like in order for sensation to be practically valuable." Menn, *Descartes and Augustine*, 230n26.

114. Menn, *Descartes and Augustine*, 223–24.

similarly take their dreams to be truthful while they are occurring.[115] Descartes cuts readers off at the pass who believe waking up definitively removes them from the illusory world of dreams as reasonableness definitively removed them from the delusional world of the madman. He writes, "[T]here are never any sure signs by means of which being awake can be distinguished from being asleep."[116] The "sure" is important here, for once again, Descartes is not saying that we can never know that we are not dreaming but if unwarily assenting, one might as well be dreaming. Descartes wants to raise the reader's alertness to the unwary form of assenting that comes naturally to him or her. If alert, we can, as Menn states, "free ourselves from our habitual criteria of judgment" and, ultimately, "isolate a genuinely sufficient criterion of truth."[117]

Descartes goes on to consider some other contenders for secure foundations but finds them all wanting. For instance, he is impressed that "whether . . . awake or asleep . . . two and three added together are five," but he realizes that God, who has allowed him to be wrong on many things in life, might let him go wrong on something as seemingly clear as 2+3=5.[118] Strikingly, Descartes declares,

> I . . . am finally compelled to admit that there is not one of my former beliefs about which a doubt may not properly be raised . . . . So in [the] future I must withhold my assent from these former beliefs just as carefully as I would from obvious falsehoods, if I want to discover any certainty.[119]

This passage is at once disturbing and promising. The reader who joins Descartes in admitting that all of his or her beliefs can be doubted sees their world view jeopardized. Yet at the same time, a more secure approach has been outlined, which might finally

---

115. Wagner, *Squaring the Circle*, 52.

116. Descartes, *Meditations*, 2:13 [VII 19].

117. Menn, *Descartes and Augustine*, 230.

118. Descartes, *Meditations*, 2:14 [VII 20].

119. Descartes, *Meditations*, 2:14–15 [VII 21–22].

find something "stable and likely to last." In the spirit of drama, however, a setback occurs.

Like Augustine in Book VII of the *Confessions*, Descartes slips back into old ways of thinking: "My habitual opinions keep coming back, and . . . they capture my belief, which is as it were bound over to them as a result of long occupation and the law of custom."[120] He then hatches a plan to remedy the situation, which contains his second most well-known statement, next to "I think, therefore I am." He writes, "I will suppose . . . that . . . some malicious demon of the utmost power and cunning has employed all his energies in order to deceive me."[121] The malicious demon is better known in popular culture by one of the other translations it has been given: the evil genius. It will be referred to hereafter simply as the demon. Crucial in Descartes's statement is the word "suppose"; the demon is conjured up to make a point. The range of the demon's deception is unsettling, for it has hypothetically deceived Descartes not only about the objects external to him but even his eyes, hands, and senses in general. The engulfing character of the demon's deception gives a hint about the point Descartes is using it to make—"that we may be at the mercy of a blind natural process which cannot do otherwise than it does," as Menn states.[122] Descartes breaks with the investigation to make an admission. He writes, "I am like a prisoner who is enjoying an imaginary freedom while asleep."[123] Nostalgia for ignorance is something the reader might experience, too, at this point, after walking down so many paths with dead-ends. Descartes is forthright about the situation, referring, in the last sentence of the First Meditation, to "the inextricable darkness of the problems . . . raised."[124] This is a frightening note to end on, especially in the context of private engagement. However, the statement also functions as a kind of cliff-hanger;

120. Descartes, *Meditations*, 2:15 [VII 22].

121. Descartes, *Meditations*, 2:15 [VII 22].

122. Menn, *Descartes and Augustine*, 242.

123. Descartes, *Meditations*, 2:15 [VII 23].

124. Descartes, *Meditations*, 2:15 [VII 23].

with more meditations to follow, a solution is anticipated, even though there seems to be no way out.[125]

The Second Meditation is entitled, "The nature of the human mind, and how it is better known than the body." Descartes states that "yesterday's meditation" has left him feeling like he is in a "deep whirlpool," but he will nevertheless "attempt the same path."[126] That path involves setting aside "[a]nything which admits of the slightest doubt" in the hopes of finding "just one thing, however slight, that is certain and unshakeable."[127] He gives a list of things he has set aside, including his memory, his senses, his body, shape, and extension. Descartes then asks if doubt can be extended to the furthest length possible: "Does it now follow that I too do not exist?"[128] He reintroduces the demon[129] to see if it could bring about an affirmative answer to this question—and it does not. Of all the candidates considered, the "I" seems immune to the demon. Descartes writes, "[L]et him deceive me as much as he can, he will never bring it about that I am nothing so long as I think that I am something."[130] Stemming from this, Descartes writes, "I must finally conclude that this proposition, *I am, I exist*, is necessarily true whenever it is put forward by me or conceived in my mind."[131] This statement obliges special consideration in light of the topic of conversion.

In the arc of conversion, the statement above marks the penultimate step in rising action; it is not the climax. The basis for

---

125. In terms of the reader's schedule of engaging the *Meditations*, Descartes states that he would "like" for a person to "devote several months, or at least weeks, to considering the topics dealt with [in the First Meditation], before going on." That this is only a recommendation seems clear from the hypothetical phrasing of his subsequent remark: "If they do this they will . . . derive much greater benefit from what follows." Descartes, *Meditations*, 2:94 [130].

126. Descartes, *Meditations*, 2:16 [VII 23–24].

127. Descartes, *Meditations*, 2:16 [VII 24].

128. Descartes, *Meditations*, 2:16 [VII 25].

129. Wagner, *Squaring the Circle*, 79n15.

130. Descartes, *Meditations*, 2:17 [VII 25].

131. Descartes, *Meditations*, 2:17 [VII 25]. Italics in the original.

reserving the label of conversion for later in the Second Meditation is twofold. First, scholars such as Hatfield and Stephen Wagner ascribe, in a word, tentativeness to the statement.[132] Second, Descartes himself conveys tentativeness by immediately admitting that he does not adequately understand "what this 'I' is."[133] He declares, "[I will] go back and meditate on what I originally believed myself to be, before I embarked on this present train of thought."[134] The purpose of going back, he explains, is to "subtract anything capable of being weakened,"[135] thus allowing him to get to the heart of what his "I" is. The process of getting to the heart of his "I" will elicit his—and his readers'—abandonment of a world view.

When Descartes outlines what he used to consider himself to be, he gives a then-uncontroversial list of things.[136] He then runs through the list looking for items that can be weakened. Descartes quickly subtracts body parts, which are plainly corporeal; however, he slows down when he gets to things formerly taken as connected in some way to the soul, such as nutrition and sense-perception. Not coincidentally, Aristotelians would include these in their conception of soul.[137] Ultimately, he subtracts them, too, leaving only one thing. Descartes writes,

> At last I have discovered it—thought; this alone is inseparable from me. I am, I exist—that is certain. But for how long? For as long as I am thinking. For it could be that were I totally to cease from thinking, I should totally cease to exist. At present I am not admitting anything except what is necessarily true. I am, then, in the strict sense only a thing that thinks; that is, I am a mind, or

132. Hatfield, *Routledge Guidebook*, 123; and Wagner, *Squaring the Circle*, 76.

133. Descartes, *Meditations*, 2:17 [VII 25].

134. Descartes, *Meditations*, 2:17 [VII 25].

135. Descartes, *Meditations*, 2:17 [VII 25].

136. Descartes, *Meditations*, 2:17–18 [VII 25–26].

137. Hatfield, *Routledge Guidebook*, 123. The understanding of sense-perception that they included but which Descartes wants to exclude—or subtract—is, as Hatfield states, "neural activity." Hatfield, *Routledge Guidebook*, 124.

intelligence, or intellect, or reason—words whose meaning I have been ignorant of until now.[138]

The reason for deeming this passage to contain conversion lies at
its very end.[139] That until this moment Descartes has been ignorant
of the meaning of words as important as *mind, intelligence, intellect,* and *reason* marks a major turning point. Suddenly, Descartes
needs to consider all things from a higher viewpoint that is purged
of sensory and imaginative influence. For most readers, even today, such an endeavor produces puzzlement: how could things that
seem to be nothing but sensible, such as the objects in Descartes's
room, be purged of sensory and imaginative influence? Descartes
gives an explanation, shortly, using a piece of wax in his room.
The need to provide an example shows a separation in the work,
albeit a brief one, between the moment of his conversion and the
moment in which it is induced in the reader.

Descartes offers a tentative description of a thing that thinks:
it is "[a] thing that doubts, understands, affirms, denies, is willing,
is unwilling, and also imagines and has sensory perceptions."[140] He
quickly clarifies that he is considering the power of imagination
and the experience of having sensory perceptions, for the reader
might think that he has dropped his commitment to doubt all
things except one. He then reveals a lingering feeling that bodies
are known more distinctly than "this puzzling 'I' which cannot be
pictured in the imagination."[141] Plainly, he is about to tackle what
the title of the Second Meditation announces. To clear up the
matter, Descartes considers a piece of wax in front of him, which
has been taken from a honeycomb. The wax has the following
qualities: it tastes like honey, has the scent of flowers, possesses
a vivid color and shape, feels hard and cold, and makes a sound
when tapped. "[I]t has everything," comments Descartes, "which

---

138. Descartes, *Meditations*, 2:18 [VII 27].

139. Although already stated, it is worth repeating that it is Descartes the
narrator who has a conversion.

140. Descartes, *Meditations*, 2:19 [VII 28].

141. Descartes, *Meditations*, 2:20 [VII 29].

appears necessary to enable a body to be known as distinctly as possible."[142] He then puts the wax by the fire that is burning beside him. Suddenly, the taste and smell go away, the color and shape change, it feels soft and hot, and it does not make a sound when tapped. "But does the same wax remain?" asks Descartes.[143] The answer is obvious; everyone would say that it is the same wax. This compels a question: how does he know it is the same wax if all of the qualities reported by the senses have changed?

To answer the wax conundrum, Descartes employs a subtraction similar to when he wanted to determine what his "I" is. The result of the subtraction is "merely something extended, flexible and changeable."[144] As Hatfield elaborates, "[I]ts determinable spatial properties—its extension, its capacity to have a size and shape . . . remain, even when other properties, including the way in which it is extended . . . change."[145] Descartes then realizes that because the wax can be reshaped in countless ways, and the imagination cannot handle what is countless, neither the senses, as already shown, nor the imagination are providing the grounds for knowing the wax that endures. He then overcomes the conundrum:

> [T]he perception I have of [this piece of wax] is a case not of vision or touch or imagination—nor has it ever been, despite previous appearances—but of purely mental scrutiny; and this can be imperfect and confused, as it was before, or clear and distinct as it is now, depending on how carefully I concentrate on what the wax consists in.[146]

The piece of wax in Descartes's room seemed capable of being known as distinctly as possible via the deliverances of the senses, but this view is now overturned. And it is indeed the view that has been overturned, for what has unfolded is essentially a thought

---

142. Descartes, *Meditations*, 2:20 [VII 30].

143. Descartes, *Meditations*, 2:20 [VII 30].

144. Descartes, *Meditations*, 2:20 [VII 31].

145. Hatfield, *Routledge Guidebook*, 132.

146. Descartes, *Meditations*, 2:21 [VII 31].

experiment; that is, bodies are still held in doubt at this juncture.[147] As Menn explains, the goal of the wax reflection is to "undermine . . . the standard of distinctness that we take from the senses, and leave us with our intellectual self-knowledge as a new paradigm for science."[148] Put differently, the wax reflection teaches us and lets us experience what clear and distinct mental scrutiny is like.[149] Suddenly, a wellspring for a metaphysics, or First Philosophy, appears; it is one that, as Hatfield states, "would truly be a revelation" to both "the Aristotelian and the untutored person."[150] If they have cognitively imitated Descartes every step of the way, the revelation coincides with an offer of conversion. The world known through the attitude of unsophisticated empiricism is ripe for abandonment—and the basis on which one can do so supports abandoning the view that the real is fundamentally material.[151]

Descartes goes on to make another real-time reference to his room. He states that when he looks through his window, he sees men walking in the public square. But armed with the lesson learned through the wax thought experiment, he corrects himself and states that what he sees are hats and coats moving about. To say that men are walking involves going beyond hats and coats, for it could be automatons—what are today called animatronics—moving about. Descartes concludes, "[S]omething which I thought I was seeing with my eyes is in fact grasped solely by the faculty of judgement which is in my mind."[152] This statement represents

147. Hatfield, *Routledge Guidebook*, 130.

148. Menn, *Descartes and Augustine*, 258–59.

149. Hatfield, *Routledge Guidebook*, 136 and 150; Wagner, *Squaring the Circle*, 78 and 105.

150. Hatfield, *Routledge Guidebook*, 136. See also Dupré, *Passage to Modernity*, 86–88.

151. Even though the external world is still held in doubt at this point and the status of the thing that thinks as immaterial is far off from confirmation, grounds for the abandonment of materialism have been firmly established. If one accepts the discovery of the wax experiment, one cannot backtrack to the view that the senses tell the full story of reality, which materialism asserts.

152. Descartes, *Meditations*, 2:21 [VII 32]. Descartes adds that "every consideration whatsoever which contributes to my perception of the wax, or of

a kind of fork in the road, as the reader who has not grasped this aspect of him or herself cannot proceed with Descartes. The difference between the *Meditations* and a textbook is most vivid here, for no propositional statement on the page could substitute for the reader's own performance. This is why the promotion of private engagement is so vital in the *Meditations*—nobody else can cause the reader to be able to proceed.

In contrast to the "darkness" that Descartes described in the final sentence of the First Meditation, the final sentence of the Second Meditation is uplifting. He writes,

> [S]ince the habit of holding on to old opinions cannot be set aside so quickly, I should like to stop here and meditate for some time on this new knowledge I have gained, so as to fix it more deeply in my memory.[153]

It would normally be odd to deem the occurrence of the phrase "new knowledge" as momentous in a philosophical work, but it is an apt adjective here. The reader who has cognitively imitated Descartes in a serious fashion has also acquired this new knowledge and can start over—such imitation, as well as private engagement, now minimized in importance.[154] Paul S. MacDonald precisely

---

any other body, cannot but establish even more effectively the nature of my own mind." Descartes, *Meditations*, 2:22 [VII 33].

153. Descartes, *Meditations*, 2:23 [VII 34].

154. In terms of private engagement, the reader is still meditating with Descartes, thus he or she cannot "relax . . . concentration." Descartes, *Meditations*, 2:32 [VII 47]. However, to relax at this stage would only mark a momentary fall back into unwary knowing, not a total immersion in it, since the dedicated reader has fixed "deeply in . . . memory" the knowledge gained in the Second Meditation. Descartes, *Meditations*, 2:23 [VII 34]. In terms of cognitive imitation, Wagner explains that starting in the Third Meditation, Descartes leads the reader "to validate the reliability of [his or her] newly discovered capacity," namely, "to clearly and distinctly perceive." Wagner, *Squaring the Circle*, 42. The descriptor "validate" is helpful because it captures the sense in which one is no longer imitating Descartes's thoughts so as to uncover the basis for an elevated viewpoint. The reader still follows Descartes, but he or she is not as dependent as in the First and Second Meditation.

sums up what is taking place: "the reader is asked . . . to *turn away* from the old world and *turn towards* the new one."[155]

155. MacDonald, "Philosophical Conversion," 311–12. Italics in the original. Elsewhere, he describes the opening of the Third Meditation as "a *hinge* in the entire structure of the *Meditations*." MacDonald, *Descartes and Husserl*, 169. Italics in the original.

3

Conversion in Chapters 1 to 11 of Bernard Lonergan's *Insight*

Background

BERNARD LONERGAN WAS BORN on December 17, 1904 in Buckingham, Quebec.[1] Lonergan's father, Gerald, worked as a land surveyor, and his mother, Josephine, was a homemaker. Lonergan had two brothers, Gregory and Mark, and he was the eldest. Since Gerald was frequently out of town for work, Lonergan was raised primarily by his mother and her sister, Mary, who they called Aunt Minnie. In his biography of Lonergan, William Mathews reports that with a father often away, and having younger brothers, Lonergan played a more substantial role in his family than adolescents normally would.

From age six to thirteen, Lonergan attended an elementary school run by the Brothers of Christian Instruction. Established in France, the Brothers are a Catholic educational organization with a presence in Canada and other countries. The organization's motto is "God Alone." As Richard Liddy highlights, classes at the school contained students in multiple grades, allowing Lonergan

---

1. This biographical section draws extensively from Liddy, *Transforming Light*; and Mathews, *Lonergan's Quest*.

to hear material from higher grades being taught. This may have bolstered Lonergan's potential for writing a conversion work, for such a work requires simultaneously occupying different levels of personal development.

Between 1918 and 1922, Lonergan attended the Jesuit-run high school and junior college of Loyola in Montreal. As a boarder at the school, Lonergan gained exposure to Ignatian patterns of living. In his second year, the question of a vocation arose. Lonergan contemplated joining the Brothers of Christian Instruction, who oversaw the elementary school he attended, but he ultimately chose the Society of Jesus.

Lonergan entered the Jesuit Novitiate in 1922, commencing an educational journey that would span many years. The first phase involved four years at what is now known as the Ignatius Jesuit Centre in Guelph, Ontario. Importantly, Mathews claims the "most significant event in Bernard's first year" was his completion of a thirty-day retreat based on the *Spiritual Exercises*.[2] The remaining phases of education included four years of overlapping study at Heythrop College and the University of London; three years teaching at Loyola in Montreal, which he had attended himself; four years of theological studies at the Gregorian University in Rome;[3] a one-year Tertianship in France; and two years of doctoral studies in theology back at the Gregorian University. During this long period, Lonergan was ordained, but he did not finish his PhD in theology. In May of 1940, two days before his PhD defense was to occur, he was brought back to Canada due to the Second World War. It was not until 1946 that his defense finally occurred, and it took place in Montreal rather than Rome.

In the course of his formation and education in Guelph, London, Montreal, France, and Rome, Lonergan naturally gained exposure to a host of works, some of which would have a lasting

2. Mathews, *Lonergan's Quest*, 29.

3. Lonergan's superiors originally sent him to Rome with the plan that after basic theological studies he would complete a doctorate in philosophy. When they decided he should eventually teach at the Gregorian, a doctorate in theology became the goal, for the theology program was known to feature mainly English-speaking students. See Lonergan, *Grace and Freedom*, xvii–xviii.

influence on him. Among them were works by Augustine of Hippo, John Alexander Stuart, John Henry Newman, and Christopher Dawson. Mathews reports that in hindsight, Lonergan described the manner in which certain books turned up at significant moments in his life as "providence."[4] What is unique about Lonergan's education is the minimal role Thomas Aquinas played at the outset. Eventually, Lonergan did focus on Aquinas, writing his dissertation on Aquinas's account of grace. In addition to Aquinas, Lonergan gained exposure to the thought of Joseph Maréchal. Maréchal was a Belgian philosopher who tried to reconcile the thought of Aquinas with that of the German philosopher Immanuel Kant.

In 1940, Lonergan began a phase of teaching theology in Canada that would last thirteen years. He taught first in Montreal, and then in Toronto at Regis College. While at the latter he began writing *Insight: A Study of Human Understanding*.[5]

In 1953, Lonergan was somewhat abruptly transferred to teach at the Gregorian University in Rome, where he had studied for the doctorate. This meant that he had to finish his work on *Insight* sooner than he preferred. He completed *Insight* that year, but the publisher requested revisions—something he would carry out while teaching in Rome. *Insight* was finally published in 1957.

As announced at the outset of this book, Lonergan's post-*Insight* life will not be reviewed in detail. It can simply be stated that Lonergan continued teaching until 1965, when he was diagnosed with cancer and had to leave Rome. After undergoing surgery, he returned to teaching, in North York and Boston. He also continued to write, publishing *Method in Theology* in 1973—a work that tackled what he had hoped to provide at the end of *Insight*. His recognition grew in this period: he received mention in *Time* magazine in 1970 and was invested as Companion of the Order of Canada the following year. In 1983, he was again diagnosed with cancer and passed away on November 26, 1984.

---

4. Mathews, *Lonergan's Quest*, 20.

5. For the sequence in which chapters of *Insight* were written, see Mathews, *Lonergan's Quest*, 10.

Insight as a Conversion Work

As the index to Bernard Lonergan's *Insight: A Study of Human Understanding* attests, the word *conversion* only appears twice in the work.[6] In both instances, the term refers to religious conversion. When the meaning of conversion is expanded to include what this book means by it, the infrequency is ironic; conversion lies at the very heart of the work.

Insight is divided into two parts: "Insight as Activity," which spans ten chapters, and "Insight as Knowledge," which spans ten chapters and an epilogue. It is the first part and the first chapter of the second part that are of primary interest for the purposes of this book.

In the Introduction to *Insight*, Lonergan writes, "[T]he aim of the work is to convey an insight into insight."[7] This statement is clarified by Lonergan's basic description of insight: "An insight is no more than an act of understanding."[8] Thus the aim of the work, alternatively stated, is to convey "an understanding of understanding."[9] The rationale for this aim is at once obvious and elusive. If one looks around the room one is in and claims to understand everything going on in the room, there is still one thing left to understand: one's own understanding. Lonergan believes that it is not worthwhile to sharpen one's understanding of things if one has not first sharpened the understanding instrument. Consider the following illustration of insight: "[a] prisoner wishing to escape sees a few loose bricks, a plank of wood, and a piece of rope and says, 'An escape route!'"[10] One could have sharp vision of these objects for weeks without realizing their capacity for escape; only sharp understanding can provide that.

It is important to note that Lonergan is by no means the first thinker to study understanding. To give just two examples,

---

6. Lonergan, *Insight*, 15 and 764.

7. Lonergan, *Insight*, 4.

8. Lonergan, *Insight*, 69.

9. Lonergan, *Insight*, 398n21.

10. This illustration is given in Fitzpatrick, *Philosophical Encounters*, 40.

Scottish philosopher David Hume sought to "enquire seriously into the nature of human understanding,"[11] and Kant wanted to carry out "[a] dissection of the faculty of the understanding itself."[12] *Insight* is a contribution to this long-standing conversation.

Lonergan goes on to elucidate the aim of *Insight*: "to assist the reader in effecting a personal appropriation of the concrete dynamic structure immanent and recurrently operative in his own cognitional activities."[13] This enterprise, which Lonergan names "self-appropriation," involves managing a structure that Lonergan believes to exist, even if unexercised, within cognitional process. Now, to help the reader manage something within him or herself evidently involves inducing significant change in the reader. As he explains, "[S]elf-appropriation . . . is a development of the subject and in the subject, and like all development it can be solid and fruitful only by being painstaking and slow."[14] Significant change is one thing, however; it is another thing to claim—as this chapter will—that the result of self-appropriation is a conversion. Recall here the definition of conversion that this book operates with: to abandon a world view and start over.[15] Evidence of the second element, starting over, is found in the Introduction. About self-appropriation, Lonergan writes, "Up to that decisive achievement all leads. From it all follows."[16] And he goes on to state that self-appropriation "is not an end in itself but rather a beginning."[17] These statements alone legitimate further exploration of conversion in *Insight*, especially as it pertains to the first element: abandoning a world view.

11. Hume, *Enquiry Concerning Human Understanding*, 8 [I.12.12].

12. Kant, *Critique of Pure Reason*, 103 [B90]. Italics removed.

13. Lonergan, *Insight*, 11.

14. Lonergan, *Insight*, 17.

15. This definition is adapted from MacDonald, "Philosophical Conversion," 304.

16. Lonergan, *Insight*, 13.

17. Lonergan, *Insight*, 22.

A Map of Conversion in *Insight*

Insight contains conversion in two respects. First, *Insight* contains a systematic expression of a conversion in chapter 11, which is entitled "The Self-affirmation of the Knower." There Lonergan affirms that the structure he has theorized to exist within his cognitional activities is in fact real, and he commits to adhere to its norms and implications for the remainder of the work. Suffice it to say, at this juncture, the implications are substantial enough to at least entertain the designation *conversion*. It must be noted that in deeming his analysis of cognitional process as correct, Lonergan is making a judgment, and a judgment goes beyond understanding to knowing. *Insight*, then, is ultimately about knowing, not simply understanding. The reason he gives understanding special emphasis is that it plays a vital role in knowing—a vital role he believes a great many thinkers have neglected. As already mentioned, a jagged understanding instrument will, in Lonergan's view, produce a jagged judgment, including a jagged judgment about what constitutes a knower. A lucid expression of this point is found in his 1958 seminar on *Insight*.[18] Lonergan remarks,

> The trick in self-appropriation is to move one step backwards, to move into the subject as intelligent—asking questions; as having insights—being able to form concepts; as weighing the evidence—being able to judge. . . .
> The first part of insight is primarily concerned with moving in there. In the second part we begin to draw conclusions, and that is where the arguable issues arise. But there is very little point to the argument unless one has been in there.[19]

18. Lonergan's *Understanding and Being* is a corrected transcription of the seminar, which took place at Saint Mary's University, Halifax. Appealing to this text here and below marks an exception to this book's endeavor—noted in the Introduction—to interpret the works under consideration through their own parameters. However, since the seminar was conducted only one year after the publication of *Insight*, it seems an acceptable exception.

19. Lonergan, *Understanding and Being*, 14 and 17. Trail offs in the original.

To say that one must go to a place within one's thinking, what in *Insight* Lonergan calls "advertence to what is happening in oneself when . . . insight occurs,"[20] sets the work apart from a textbook. *Insight* is set even further apart when Lonergan goes on to highlight the necessity of "pulling out . . . inadequate ideals [of knowledge]."[21] There is a kind of cleansing, not entirely different from that found in Ignatius's *Spiritual Exercises*, that one must put one's cognitional activities through before one can start to gain secure knowledge.[22] Whereas in a textbook readers cannot turn to page two unless they have assented to the knowledge offered on page one, in *Insight* readers cannot turn a page unless they have uprooted inadequate ideals of knowledge peculiar to themselves. The upshot of this is that "self-appropriation . . . will not be the same for everyone."[23] This statement evinces the fact that *Insight* is a record of Lonergan's own conversion. While Lonergan lays out a wide range of inadequate ideals and blockades to the immanent structure, these are nevertheless his own conceptions of the matter. One must not let the pedagogical and systematic characteristics of the first part of *Insight* and chapter 11 lead to the belief that Lonergan is telling one's own story. As will be explained, to fall into that trap would be to miss a genuine conversion.

The second sense in which *Insight* contains conversion is more explicitly autobiographical. In the Introduction, Lonergan speaks of two realisms, "an incoherent realism, half animal and half human, . . . and . . . an intelligent and reasonable realism."[24] According to both of these perspectives, our ideas about the world are not just in our heads, hence the term *realism*. However, the sense in which our ideas are not just in our heads differs, with the former taking a match between idea and world to be immediate and the later taking a match to be mediated. More will be

---

20. Lonergan, *Understanding and Being*, 21.

21. Lonergan, *Understanding and Being*, 17–18.

22. Lonergan, *Insight*, 17. Elizabeth Murray outlines additional parallels. See Murray, "Bernard Lonergan."

23. Lonergan, *Understanding and Being*, 18.

24. Lonergan, *Insight*, 22.

said about this in due course. What is important at this point is Lonergan's ensuing claim about the two realisms: "the discovery" of them is so momentous that "one has not made it yet if one has no clear memory of its startling strangeness."[25] Plainly, Lonergan himself has a clear memory of having discovered the two realisms. What the definitive article before "discovery" and subsequent use of the pronoun "one" imply is that it is not something only Lonergan has had or can have.

Lonergan goes on to use an allegory to describe his own—and potentially others'—shift from subscribing to the first realism to the second.[26] Lonergan's phrasing of the allegory, which has to do with residing in halfway houses during a journey, is sufficiently tricky to warrant appeal to another source. As Mark Morelli explains, the allegory revolves around the two previously discussed realisms and three philosophical doctrines: materialism, idealism, and critical realism. Morelli contends that the idealism being referred to is German philosopher Georg Hegel's absolute idealism, not Kant's critical idealism—even though *Insight* as a whole is a response to both.[27] Briefly, materialism is the view that the real is fundamentally material, idealism is the view that the real is fundamentally mental or spiritual, and critical realism is the view that "the real . . . is whatever is to be grasped intelligently and affirmed reasonably."[28] Lonergan's claim is that people who have difficulties with materialism but also with idealism settle into a halfway house that is a compromise between the two: an incoherent realism.[29] Those who advance to critical realism and embrace an intelligent and reasonable realism see idealism as a halfway house.[30]

Liddy and Mathews contend that Lonergan's halfway house allegory is autobiographical.[31] Liddy writes,

25. Lonergan, *Insight*, 22.

26. Lonergan, *Insight*, 22.

27. Morelli, "Going Beyond Idealism," 311 and 325.

28. Lonergan, *Insight*, 540.

29. Morelli, "Going Beyond Idealism," 316.

30. Morelli, "Going Beyond Idealism," 316.

31. Liddy, *Transforming Light*, xviii and 37; and Mathews, *Lonergan's Quest*,

As a student in England in the late 1920s, Lonergan rejected a version of scholastic realism and, under the influence of English empirical thought, he identified himself as a "nominalist." Later, after reading Plato and Augustine, he came to a "theory of intellect as immanent act" and, as he later confessed, experienced the fear of becoming an idealist. Finally, under the influence of the Jesuit writers, Joseph Maréchal and Bernard Leeming, he came to realize [in the mid-1930s] the meaning of the scholastic teaching on the "real distinction between essence and existence," and that was the key to what he later called his own intellectual conversion to a "critical realism."[32]

Three points of clarification must be made here. First, while Lonergan was never a materialist, the doctrine has a philosophical affinity with nominalism, which Lonergan did subscribe to. Second, although the passage above only speaks of fearing of becoming an idealist, Morelli contends that Lonergan did temporarily adopt the (absolute) idealist viewpoint. Morelli goes on to claim that "passage through the halfway house of idealism on the way to critical realism is conditionally necessary."[33] He explains that Hegel rejects "the ideal of immediate confrontation with the real,"[34] and this rejection is essential for progression to critical realism. Third, Lonergan's mid-1930s conversion is distinct from the conversion expressed in *Insight*. When Lonergan commences the section on the self-affirmation of the knower in chapter 11, he writes, "'Am I a knower?' Each has to ask the question of himself."[35] The answer Lonergan supplies to this question in *Insight* is far more comprehensive than what he would have given in the 1930s. Following

---

72, 162, and 453.

32. Liddy, *Transforming Light*, xviii.

33. Morelli, "Going Beyond Idealism," 318–19 and 328. Capitalization of "Critical Realism" removed.

34. Morelli, "Going Beyond Idealism," 322.

35. Lonergan, *Insight*, 352.

the practice of the preceding chapters of this book, what follows examines the ideal answer to the question—that found in *Insight*.[36]

Even though the startling strangeness occurred in the 1930s, Lonergan has, as Liddy puts it, "invited others, in *Insight*, to share in that breakthrough."[37] This statement prompts a return to the topic of *Insight*'s induction of conversion; Lonergan encourages the reader to share in his overcoming of the doctrines of materialism and idealism, as well as an incoherent realism that resides between them. The way that Lonergan encourages this is not simply by formulating arguments against those positions; rather, the reader is asked to inspect whether the structure immanent and recurrently operative in Lonergan's cognitional activities is also immanent and recurrently operative in his or her own cognitional activities. If it is, overcoming materialism, idealism, and incoherent realism becomes not just something Lonergan wants the reader to do but something the reader experiences him or herself as needing to do.

Before proceeding, a clarification must be made regarding exactly what is abandoned in conversion. Recall that Lonergan plants both feet in absolute idealism before moving on to critical realism. To say that he *overcomes* that idealism is accurate, but to say that he *abandons* it is not entirely accurate. To be sure, neither Lonergan, nor the readers who follow him, are "idealists" by the end of chapter 11, yet they retain its dismissal of "the ideal of immediate confrontation with the real." The world view abandoned in chapter 11 of *Insight*, then, is that envisaged within materialism and the compromise of an incoherent realism.

Cognitive Imitation

What follows is a summary of what Lonergan lays out as the concrete dynamic structure immanent and recurrently operative in his cognitional activities. The matter-of-fact form in which Lonergan

---

36. Readers interested in analysis of Lonergan's earlier accounts of his transformation may consult Liddy, *Transforming Light*; Mathews, *Lonergan's Quest*; and Morelli, *At the Threshold*.

37. Liddy, *Transforming Light*, xix.

lays out the structure can easily lead one to forget that it is, for the reader, merely a proposal. The reader must attempt to imitate what Lonergan lays out with the aim of determining whether the structure really exists.

When Lonergan adverts to his own cognitional activities, he finds three "successive levels of consciousness."[38] The levels are: empirical consciousness, intellectual consciousness, and rational consciousness.[39] For the sake of brevity, Lonergan associates one emblematic cognitional operation with each level: experiencing, understanding, and judging/deciding.[40] He then takes up the particularities of each of these operations. With respect to experiencing, Lonergan distinguishes two types of data. A datum of sense is "the content of an act of seeing, hearing, touching, tasting, smelling."[41] The data of consciousness "consist of acts of seeing, hearing, tasting, smelling, touching, perceiving, imagining, inquiring, understanding, formulating, reflecting, judging, and so forth."[42]

What effects the transition from empirical consciousness to intellectual consciousness is inquiry. Inquiry changes the mind from being in a state of passively experiencing data to actively wondering about data. At this point, inquiry manifests itself in "questions for intelligence," such as "What? and Why? and How often?"[43] On this level, namely, understanding, there are a host of cognitional operations. The first operation is insight. Lonergan identifies two major types of insight; the more regularly occurring type is "direct insight" or "direct understanding."[44] This type of insight answers a

38. Lonergan, *Insight*, 14.

39. Lonergan, *Insight*, 14 and 346.

40. Lonergan lists the first three operations in this form in *Insight*, 757 and the fourth in *Insight*, 636. Readers of this book will notice that these and some ensuing references fall after the site of conversion, namely, after chapter 11. Unlike the *Confessions* and the *Meditations*, *Insight* is not a narrative, thus ideas are communicated more than once—often in a more quotable form.

41. Lonergan, *Insight*, 96.

42. Lonergan, *Insight*, 299.

43. Lonergan, *Insight*, 298.

44. Lonergan, *Insight*, 509. The other type is inverse insight. Lonergan

question for intelligence. The second operation is conception. In conception, "insights . . . are expressed or formulated in concepts, suppositions, definitions, postulates, hypotheses, theories."[45] An insight can be expressed in a simple concept, such as "The king," or in a complex concept, such as "The king is dead." In the latter example, the "is" is merely the "is" of synthesis; the synthesis is not being posited. One has a prospective judgment in mind, but as a conception, it is "simply an object of thought."[46] The third and final operation is reflective understanding; it "grasps the sufficiency of the evidence for a prospective judgment."[47] Reflective understanding sifts through the data of sense, the products of the imagination, and the direct insight.[48]

Advancing to rational consciousness, Lonergan states that on this level inquiry manifests itself in "question[s] for reflection," such as "Is it so?"[49] A judgment changes a conception from an object of thought into an object of affirmation[50] or an object of negation.[51] Lonergan holds that a range of answers are possible to a question for reflection: "You do not *have* to say yes or no; you can say, 'I don't know.' You do not *have* to say, 'It certainly is so'; you can say, 'It probably is so' or 'It possibly is so.'"[52] The answer one selects from this list depends in part upon whether the insight under consideration is vulnerable or invulnerable. "[A]n insight is . . . invulnerable," writes Lonergan, "if there are no further pertinent questions."[53] Otherwise, an insight is vulnerable. In the in-

explains, "While direct insight grasps the point, or sees the solution . . . , inverse insight apprehends that . . . there is no point, or that the solution is to deny a solution." Lonergan, *Insight*, 44.

45. Lonergan, *Insight*, 278.

46. Lonergan, *Insight*, 296.

47. Lonergan, *Insight*, 304.

48. Mathews, *Lonergan's Quest*, 170.

49. Lonergan, *Insight*, 304.

50. Lonergan, *Insight*, 695.

51. Lonergan, *Insight*, 457.

52. Lonergan, *Understanding and Being*, 113. Italics added for clarity. See also Lonergan, *Insight*, 297.

53. Lonergan, *Insight*, 312.

vulnerable scenario, "judgments are obviously certain," but in the vulnerable scenario, "judgments are at best probable."[54]

At this point, one would be right to think that not enough has been said about the structure immanent and recurrently operative in Lonergan's cognitional activities to warrant his—or potentially the reader's—abandonment of any sophisticated world view. The full basis for abandonment is bound up with what Lonergan names the "pure, detached, disinterested desire . . . to know."[55] There are several features of the desire to know that must be outlined.

To begin, the desire to know is opposed to the interference of bias. Lonergan distinguishes several types of bias: avoiding data that might bring about an unwanted insight, blocking further relevant questions from consideration, limiting understanding to what keeps one's group in power, and restricting knowing to what works.[56]

The desire to know is also opposed to the inhibitions of cognitional process that arise from other human desires and drives.[57] This is connected to Lonergan's view that the flow of consciousness—that is, the flow of sensations, images, emotions, and bodily movements—can be in a certain pattern: "biological, aesthetic, artistic, dramatic, practical, intellectual, or mystical."[58] Within the biological pattern, the flow is governed by an interest in self-preservation and reproduction. The general outlook within this pattern is "extroversion," which is a concern with "external conditions and opportunities."[59] Here, an object is real to the extent that it satiates one's biological needs. Such an object is a "body," an "already out there now real."[60] By contrast, the intellectual pat-

54. Lonergan, *Insight*, 325.

55. Lonergan, *Insight*, 97.

56. Lonergan, *Insight*, 214–31 and 244–67.

57. Lonergan, *Insight*, 404.

58. Lonergan, *Insight*, 410.

59. Lonergan, *Insight*, 207.

60. Lonergan, *Insight*, 276. Interestingly, Lonergan's very first use of the term *body* in *Insight* is in connection with Augustine of Hippo: "it took him years to make the discovery that the name 'real' might have a different connotation from the name 'body.'" Lonergan, *Insight*, 15. For Augustine's influence

tern of experience opposes restrictions on its interests. In this pattern, "the real is being; it is whatever is to be grasped intelligently and affirmed reasonably."[61] An object from the perspective of this pattern is not a "body," but a "thing."[62] Lonergan maintains that one cannot completely escape the biological pattern, thus the solution to the problem is not the elimination of that pattern. Rather, one must "acknowledge the reality of the various blends and mixtures of the patterns of human experience, and . . . grasp how these blends and mixtures generate confusion and error on the notions of reality, objectivity, and knowledge."[63] Objectivity is conceived of as a matter of extroversion when an indiscriminate blending of the biological and intellectual patterns takes place.

Finally, the desire to know reaches beyond the subject to what is. Lonergan ultimately upholds "the traditional definition of truth as the conformity or correspondence of the subject's affirmations and negations to what is and is not."[64] This brings some clarification to the sense in which, for Lonergan, our ideas about the world are not just in our heads.

Having delineated the structure immanent and recurrently operative in his cognitional activities, as well as the driving force behind it, Lonergan moves, in chapter 11, to affirm that he is a knower. In order to move from the claim "these cognitional acts regularly occur" to the claim "these cognitional acts make me a knower," Lonergan invokes a retortion argument.[65] The argument is that his account of knowing "is not open to revision in any concrete meaning of the term 'revision' [since] any human reviser would appeal to experience, understanding, and judgment."[66] The phrase "any human reviser" is critical. By this point in chapter 11,

---

on Lonergan, see Liddy, *Transforming Light*, 50–73.

61. Lonergan, *Insight*, 520.

62. Lonergan, *Insight*, 275.

63. Lonergan, *Insight*, 607.

64. Lonergan, *Insight*, 575.

65. Lonergan, *Insight*, 359–60. Martin Moleski has composed a history of the argument and offers reflections on its use by Lonergan. See Moleski, "Retortion," 63–66; and Moleski, "The Role of Retortion," 225–31, respectively.

66. Lonergan, *Insight*, 757.

Lonergan is confident that he has shone a bright enough light on the reader's experiencing, understanding, and judging, and their relations, that he or she cannot reject that structure without being aware of the contradiction involved in doing so. It is acceptable to think "Smith never thinks anything" except if you are Smith.[67] It is also acceptable to think "Lonergan is wrong about human knowing" except if you read his account, understood what he meant by it, and judged it to be false. Lonergan admits that the reader's account of knowing might "be said more accurately and more fully," but a refined version would still be the fruit of the structure Lonergan has outlined.[68]

A Concrete Example

It is prudent to provide an example of cognitional structure in action. Lonergan himself provides examples, such as during his analysis of the definition of a circle,[69] but they often lack one or more of the elements outlined above. What follows is a unique example that captures as many elements outlined above as possible.[70]

In the television game show *Liars Club*, four celebrities sit at a panel on one side of the set, and four contestants sit at a panel on the other side.[71] A peculiar item is given to the celebrities; for instance, a motorized propeller with backpack-like arm straps. Each celebrity gives a different account of what the item is. The contestants, who silently look at the item from a distance, must ultimately place a bet on the one celebrity they judge to be telling the

---

67. This example is adapted from Hugo Meynell. See Meynell, *Redirecting Philosophy*, 9.

68. Lonergan, *Understanding and Being*, 144.

69. The circle exercise is found in Lonergan, *Insight*, 31–37.

70. Other concrete examples can be found in the work of Frank Budenholzer and Patrick Byrne. See, for example, Budenholzer, "Emergence, Probability, and Reductionism"; and Byrne, "Statistics as Science."

71. The details provided here pertain to the 1976–1979 run of the show. For background information, see Schwartz et al., *Encyclopedia of TV Game Shows*, 127–28.

truth. As the first celebrity tells a story about the item and points to its various features to substantiate the story, the contestants are collecting data of sense. At some point during the story, the celebrity supplies an answer to the question for intelligence, "What is it?" For instance, the celebrity states that the motorized propeller with backpack-like arm straps is a device that people hang gliding wear to help them steer as they glide. This becomes a prospective judgment in the mind of each contestant. As an object of thought, the statement merely rests in the contestant's consciousness; it is not yet affirmed or negated. Three more possible answers to the question, "What is it?" are still to be presented by the celebrities.

Once all four of the celebrities have supplied their stories, the contestants must review the data of sense that they have collected and determine which answer to the question "What is it?" has the most corroboration from those data. That is, they must have an act of reflective understanding. In the rare case of a contestant who has real-world experience with an item, his or her insight into it is invulnerable. Normally, however, the contestants must work with a vulnerable insight. The frustration at not being able to ask questions is something the contestants and viewers share.

Let us assume one contestant takes the answer "The item is a hang glider's backpack propeller" to be most corroborated by the data. This contestant can turn this object of thought into an object of affirmation by answering the question for reflection, "Is it so?" In the rare case that the contestant's insight is invulnerable, he or she can answer, "It certainly is so" and wager a large amount of money. Otherwise, the contestant has to work with the answer "It probably is so" and wager an amount that matches his or her degree of certainty. Assessing that degree might involve a return to the levels of empirical and intellectual consciousness. Contestants who return to intellectual consciousness must not let an external opportunity, namely, the prospect of winning more money from a bigger wager, cloud the assessment. Furthermore, they must not let the bias of being starstruck with a particular celebrity influence their degree of certainty.

In some cases, there is a commercial break before the truth is revealed. That television viewers stay tuned during the commercial break demonstrates the existence of an unrestricted desire to know, for they do not earn any money by being correct.[72]

Once the truthful celebrity is revealed, the contestants' money totals are adjusted accordingly. The celebrities then move on to another item. At the end of the show, the contestant with the greatest amount of money wins. Generally speaking, the winner is the contestant who judges most closely in accord with the evidence and who exercises the most prudence in affixing a degree of certitude to his or her judgments.

Private Engagement

What remains to be discussed is the environment in which *Insight* is to be engaged. Lonergan describes chapters 1 to 11 of *Insight*, which contain the arc of conversion, as "[an] experiment . . . performed not publicly but privately."[73] There are three senses in which the experiment is performed privately. First, as Liddy explains, the experiment "takes place in the hiddenness of one's presence to oneself."[74] This point is rather straightforward; others do not have access to one's cognitional process. The second sense of private engagement is embedded in this passage from *Insight*:

> Deep within us all, emergent when the noise of other appetites is stilled, there is a drive to know, to understand, to see why, to discover the reason, to find the cause, to explain. . . . It can absorb a man. It can keep him for hours, day after day, year after year, in the narrow prison of his study or his laboratory.[75]

---

72. In the context of this game show, there is an additional element involved in judgment: trust in the producers. The contestants assume that the producers are being honest when they reveal which celebrity has not been lying.

73. Lonergan, *Insight*, 13.

74. Liddy, *Transforming Light*, 107.

75. Lonergan, *Insight*, 28.

This passage is autobiographical; it details the conditions under which *Insight* was authored.[76] The book was written in a small room in Toronto and involved—as one might expect from a work over 700 pages in length—intense focus. Since *Insight* is a record of self-appropriation, and writing down that self-appropriation involved being in solitude, it is reasonable to infer that the ideal condition for reading the work is also in solitude. The third and final sense of private engagement is bound up with Lonergan's delineation of patterns of experience. The self-affirmation of the knower occurs within the intellectual pattern of experience. Lonergan acknowledges that "no one remains in [the intellectual pattern] permanently," but one can subdue the other patterns long enough to carry out the self-affirmation.[77] If the intellectual pattern is not dominant, "the self of our self-affirmation seems quite different from one's actual self."[78] The dramatic pattern, which handles "dealing with other persons," is among the patterns to be subdued.[79] It follows that one must not be dealing with other persons or thinking about dealing with other persons when the self-affirmation takes place in chapter 11. Beyond this point, with the "experiment" having been performed, the importance of private engagement is minimized.

Further Mapping Conversion in *Insight*

Occurring in solitude, and completely one's own possession, the self-affirmation of the knower grants a person "a basis within himself . . . to which he can appeal in the last resort."[80] Lonergan is speaking in general here, but his statement is especially relevant to the topic of conversion. Recall that Lonergan wants to share his

76. Mathews, *Lonergan's Quest*, 3–4.

77. Lonergan, *Insight*, 411. When the "intellectual drive is dominant," one becomes "an incarnation of inquiring intelligence." Lonergan, *Insight*, 97.

78. Lonergan, *Insight*, 410. Indentation removed.

79. Lonergan, *Insight*, 495. Strictly speaking, when one "refuses even to face others," it is still a use of the dramatic pattern. Lonergan, *Insight*, 495.

80. Lonergan, *Understanding and Being*, 35.

experience of "startling strangeness" with the reader of *Insight*, which is the experience of discovering the mediated form of a match between idea and world. It is startling since, for those who have long assumed such a match to be immediate, the world is no longer "out there." For such persons, this constitutes the most fundamental world view challenge possible; the presumption of a world "out there" is more basic than, as well as an element of, materialism. With a fundamental world view in jeopardy, one is in a last resort scenario. In such a scenario, the only basis for objection is one's own experience of knowing. But by chapter 11 of *Insight*, Lonergan has cast such a bright light on the process of knowing that one has virtually no room for objecting. This point is embedded in Lonergan's statement that *Insight* contains "a series of exercises in self-appropriation, in reaching . . . functionally operative tendencies."[81] *Insight* slowly illuminates and sharpens these tendencies, such that the "startling strangeness" both occurs and is bearable. Once one abandons the assumption of a world "out there," materialism is no longer viable. It is worth noting that while the unrefined materialism that Augustine subscribed to before his conversion was no longer held by thinkers in Lonergan's time, *Insight* is a response to a refined form.[82]

In chapter 12 of *Insight*, Lonergan starts over; the project of self-appropriation "expands into a metaphysics and an ethics" and "mounts to a conception and an affirmation of God."[83] Importantly, as he proposes a metaphysics—an overarching conception of reality—he constantly stresses "the isomorphism that obtains between the structure of knowing and the structure of the known."[84]

---

81. Lonergan, *Understanding and Being*, 17.

82. In the Epilogue, Lonergan laments that "we live in the midst of a sensate culture, in which very many men, insofar as they acknowledge any hegemony of truth, give their allegiance not to a divine revelation, nor to a theology, nor to a philosophy, nor even to an intellectualist science, but to science interpreted in a positivistic and pragmatic fashion." Lonergan, *Insight*, 766.

83. Lonergan, *Insight*, 753.

84. Lonergan, *Insight*, 424.

4

Conversion in Peter Weir's
The Truman Show

Background

PETER WEIR'S 1998 FILM *The Truman Show* revolves around Truman Burbank, a man apparently unaware that he is the star of The Truman Show, a 24/7 television program.[1] Now twenty-nine years old, Truman was adopted at birth by a television corporation and raised in the fabricated town of Seahaven, which is equipped with 5,000 hidden cameras. Seahaven is housed under a giant metal dome next to the Hollywood sign in Los Angeles. The majority of the public love The Truman Show—so much so that they attend outdoor stadiums to watch special life events, such as Truman's wedding. Needless to say, everyone in Truman's life is an actor, including his wife, Meryl, and his best friend, Marlon. The show's revenue is generated through product placement; you can buy the kitchen knife that Meryl uses, the beer that Marlon drinks, and so on. The actors receive earpiece instructions from a control room located near the top of the dome, behind the moon. Christof, the

---

1. In this chapter, *The Truman Show* (italicized) refers to the film and The Truman Show (not italicized) refers to the television show within the film.

creator of The Truman Show, oversees the control room and acts as director for important moments in the show.

Since *The Truman Show* is a work of fiction, a different approach is required for exploring its status as a conversion work. In the works previously considered, it was essentially the author of the work who underwent conversion; in this work, a purely fictional character undergoes conversion. The approach required, then, is one that passes over Weir's personal background and attends instead to his declared intentions with the film.[2] One might wonder why it is Weir's intentions, rather than those of script writer Andrew Niccol, that receive attention in what follows.[3] The reason is that Niccol's draft scripts are markedly different from the script used for filming, which Weir assisted with. Contrasting Niccol's script with the shooting script, Weir commented, "Everything changed really, other than the concept and the characters."[4] Even this comment falls short of capturing his involvement, for a character, Christof, was substantially shaped by Weir.[5]

The Truman Show as a Conversion Work

Weir's high level of creative involvement in the film renders any statements he has made on or near the topic of conversion especially valuable. One such statement can be found in his 1998 interview with Shane Danielsen. While discussing *The Truman Show*, Weir remarks that he enjoys "rites-of-passage stories" because they involve "[t]he search for truth, coming to some kind

2. For interested readers, Weir discusses his background in Weir, "The Director's Voice."

3. Readers seeking insight into Niccol's background may consult King, "Director Andrew Niccol."

4. Kalina, "Designing Visions," 20. In the same interview, Weir reports that the original script underwent ten rewrites—the original being "certainly darker" and "set in New York City."

5. Bliss, "Keeping a Sense of Wonder," 7. It is worth noting that all footage of Christof was shot after Jim Carrey completed filming. Moreover, just as in the film, Ed Harris never met Carrey during production.

of self-knowledge and deeper understanding of the world."[6] These words verge upon this book's definition of conversion. To reiterate the definition, conversion means abandoning a world view and starting over.[7] On the one hand, a deeper understanding of the world requires the abandonment of an obsolete world view, and on the other, a rite of passage requires starting on a new path in life. There is a basis, then, for exploring whether *The Truman Show* contains conversion. There is also a basis for exploring whether the film induces conversion. In a 1998 interview with Michael Bliss, Weir comments that *The Truman Show* is "a movie that keeps making itself in your mind. . . . [W]hen you leave the enclosed world of the cinema and walk out into the reality of your world, you . . . step into Truman's shoes."[8] Weir's statement suggests that the viewer can undergo what Truman underwent, which in this chapter's view is conversion. The statement also intimates that such conversion appears late in the film. Specifically, it appears at the one hour and twenty-nine minute mark, which is six minutes from the end credits.[9] This contrasts with Augustine's *Confessions*, Descartes's *Meditations*, and Lonergan's *Insight*, where conversion rests roughly halfway through.

Additional grounds for labeling the film a conversion work are found in the body of texts that analyze Weir's films. One such text is by Richard Leonard; he sheds light on the way in which Weir's films transform the viewer. Leonard writes, "[Weir] leads the spectator to contemplate his or her place in a larger frame of reference where physical laws count for less and a relationship with a metaphysical . . . world . . . is taken seriously."[10] He goes on

6. Danielsen, "Back on the A-list," 6, quoted in Leonard, "Mystical Gaze," 56. Attention was drawn to this and several other interview excerpts by Leonard.

7. This definition is adapted from MacDonald, "Philosophical Conversion," 304.

8. Bliss, "Keeping a Sense of Wonder," 7.

9. This chapter utilizes a Special Edition DVD manufactured in 2010. The exact length of the film on the DVD is 1:42:50. This version continues to be available at the time of writing.

10. Leonard, "Mystical Gaze," 8.

to state that Weir "transforms the spectator's awareness . . . [and] suggests that there are realities beyond his or her sight."[11] Leonard's words support a reading of Weir's films as promoting the abandonment of materialism, albeit a less nuanced form than that abandoned in the other works considered in this book. Leonard also invokes the term *conversion* on several occasions: he notes that Danielsen found "conversion at the core" of *The Truman Show*;[12] he describes Weir's film *Witness* as "a conversion narrative;"[13] and he asserts Weir's main characters reach a state where "conversion, dread and death are not seen as loss or annihilation but experienced as illuminating and transcending."[14] Despite the absence of further treatment of the topic, Leonard's words above, and those still to be referred to in this chapter, bolster the designation of the film as a conversion work.

Another important scholarly text is by Michael Bliss, whose 1998 interview with Weir was just referred to. Similar to Leonard, Bliss finds in Weir's films the message that "what we perceive with our senses is, at best, an unreliable indication of what really exists."[15] The transformation Weir aims to bring about in viewers is "to trust our philosophical and spiritual intuition to make sense of the world."[16] Bliss's statements here—and in other instances still to be consulted—lend further credence to labeling the film a conversion work, despite any direct invocation of the term. The statements also give further corroboration to reading *The Truman Show* as endorsing the abandonment of materialism.[17]

11. Leonard, "Mystical Gaze," 8.

12. Leonard, "Mystical Gaze," 55. Danielsen's full review could not be obtained at the time of writing.

13. Leonard, "Mystical Gaze," 279.

14. Leonard, "Mystical Gaze," 70.

15. Bliss, *Dreams within a Dream*, 14.

16. Bliss, *Dreams within a Dream*, 14.

17. This chapter refrains from speculating which –ism the film points to as a replacement for materialism. One possibility, explored by Christopher Falzon, is existentialism. See Falzon, "Peter Weir's *The Truman Show*."

Cognitive Imitation

Extraordinary things are placed in front of Truman throughout *The Truman Show*. For the first half of the film, he does not give them any significant reflection. The viewer, in contrast, immediately recognizes them as extraordinary and experiences frustration at Truman for not seriously reflecting on them. In the second half of the film, Truman begins to scrutinize extraordinary things to some extent, and the viewer develops some admiration for his cognitive activity. Nevertheless, the viewer continues to be in a position of perceived cognitive superiority to Truman, for he or she knows the truth about Seahaven. The development and fate of this perceived cognitive superiority is part of a plan by Weir to induce conversion in the viewer.

Weir places extraordinary things not just in front of Truman but also in front of the viewer of *The Truman Show*. Weir does the latter knowing that some viewers—namely, candidates for conversion—will not give them a second thought. This continues until a moment near the end of the film when an extraordinary thing is placed in front of both Truman and the viewer at the same time—a thing whose extraordinary quality neither could know. When the thing is revealed as extraordinary, conversion occurs for Truman and, potentially, for the viewer. The sign of successful conversion in the viewer is the replacement of a sense of cognitive superiority over Truman with a sense of cognitive equality. Truman is suddenly a figure completely worthy of imitation. The viewer who grasps this is in a position to follow Truman in his ensuing decision to start over.

Private Engagement

One can reservedly extend Margaret Miles's description of Augustine's approach in the *Confessions* to Weir's approach in *The Truman Show*: "he always addresses the individual, alone with his private thought and memories."[18] Of course, in its initial venue,

18. Miles, "On Reading Augustine," 512.

the movie theater, persons engaging the film were not alone in the strict sense. However, as many will have experienced, when an engrossing story is combined with dimmed lights and sound that surrounds, the smallest squeak of a seat can be jarring because it reminds one that one is in public. Beyond this, the film itself dissuades conversation with other viewers. With Truman at the center of the frame for the bulk of the film, the viewer is psychically absorbed by his every move. Furthermore, when Truman encounters the thing that elicits conversion, Weir lets him engage it privately by placing the camera behind his back. Truman is left alone, as it were, in the moment in which he realizes his world view must be abandoned. The viewer who grasps the implication of this realization for his or her own life joins Truman in the moment—as if it were he and the viewer alone in the theater.

A Map of Conversion in *The Truman Show*

The analysis that follows essentially matches the chronology of the film. Since *The Truman Show* is a film "in which action [is] merely the front for ideas,"[19] to echo Danielsen, it is important to start at the beginning and tackle the film's ideas as they arise. This will be achieved by creating sections that correspond to the grouped chapters in the Special Edition DVD's "scene selection" menu. Some jumping ahead will be necessary, however—including to aspects of the climax of the film. It is thus worth reiterating the statement in this book's Introduction that the reader is presumed to have viewed the film in its entirety. Additionally, it should be stressed that what follows is not a synopsis of the film; only salient elements of the film are attended to, namely, those with a bearing on the topic of conversion.

19. Danielsen, "Back on the A-list," 3, quoted in Leonard, "Mystical Gaze," 56.

A Day in a Life; Day 10,909; Aquaphobia

In the opening shot of *The Truman Show*, Christof sits "in the sky" behind Seahaven's moon, wearing a beret of the kind that artists and other "creators" have historically worn. Weir unmistakably wants to depict Christof as godlike. As the film progresses, other godlike dimensions of the character come into view: Christof is revealed to be the architect of Seahaven, which makes him a creator on a larger scale; it is said that he has access to 5,000 cameras, giving him a kind of omniscience; and his ability to control virtually every aspect of Seahaven approaches omnipotence. Since Weir has said little about the symbolism of the characters in the film, it is a great fortune that on one occasion he spoke at length about Christof. Asked whether *The Truman Show* is a Christian parable, Weir responds:

> The film picked up metaphors as it went along. I was surprised as we began to put it together how it was relaying other meanings. I was rather more drawn to Greek legend. Christof is Zeus, in the sense that he's trying to control the mortals. In my reading, as I recall, the one thing Zeus could not do is interfere with fate. He could do other God-like things, including controlling the weather, but he cannot, as Christof/Zeus does, begin to interfere with the decisions his creature has taken, which is to leave. So Christof/Zeus crosses a line at the end and is punished for it. There are all sorts of other understandings. Somebody gave me a brilliant Buddhist one, with Christof as Siddharta's father, the King, trying to stop him leaving the garden and discovering the pain of life that lies outside the palace walls.[20]

Although Weir clearly allows for and is delighted by multiple readings of Christof, in the context of scholarly reflection on the film,

---

20. Kalina, "Designing Visions," 22. Capitalization of "God-like" in the original. Since Weir is speaking of Zeus, one would expect "godlike" here, but in the context of the question posed, "God-like" is understandable. Linda Mercadante offers reflections on Christof's implications for conceptions of God. See Mercadante, "The God behind the Screen," 13–17.

his own intentions have added import. To learn that the inspiration for Christof was Zeus, a god, rather than the God of classical theism, is not entirely surprising given Weir's personal interests. What intrigues him in "discussions about religion" are "mysteries, ambiguities, contradictions[,] . . . thinking about who we are, what we believe in."[21] In accord with this, Robert Johnston writes that Weir "has certainly not provided his viewers an explicitly Christian vision."[22] Leonard echoes Johnston's view, stating that Weir wants to explore "the more general world of the 'spiritual.'"[23] The upshot of these claims is that when approaching Weir's films, one must exercise caution in taking specific elements to point to God or the Christian religion. For instance, in the opening shot of the film, Christof is also wearing a black cassock-style top with a white, round-necked shirt exposed in rectangular form underneath it. One might suspect Weir wants viewers to think of clergy upon seeing this. In reality, as Weir divulges, Christof's attire is based on "couturiers, who are kind of quasi-artists: Armani, Karl Lagerfeld, Versace."[24] Christof's function in the film is something that will be tackled when he next appears—and that is, surprisingly, in almost an hour. What is relevant at present is the lesson of refraining from rash judgments about Christof, including about his status as a benevolent or malevolent force in the film.

The arc of conversion begins when a lamp falls from the sky and lands in front of Truman's home. While Truman himself is startled by the loud crash, his neighbor can be seen in the distance walking towards a transit bus with no concern. Truman picks up the lamp and inspects it. A piece of tape on the lamp reads "Sirius (9 Canis Major)." Perhaps, like the real Sirius, this lamp is the brightest "star" in Seahaven's firmament. Truman looks upward and sees nothing but a completely clear sky. Weir then quickly cuts to Truman driving to work, and Truman is carefree; he has not grasped the event as extraordinary. As he drives, an announcer on

21. Bliss, "Keeping a Sense of Wonder," 8.

22. Johnston, "An Exercise in Dialogue," 285.

23. Leonard, "Mystical Gaze," 66.

24. Kalina, "Designing Visions," 19.

the radio states that "an aircraft in trouble began shedding parts as it flew over Seahaven just a few moments ago." Truman accepts this with a disinterested "Uh-huh." The viewer of the film scoffs at Truman for ignoring the holes in the plane story: why would a plane light be labeled Sirius, how could the plane not be seen in a cloudless sky, and so forth. The sentiment is increased when the radio announcer asks, "Are you thinking of flying?" Truman replies, "Nope." The announcer responds, "Good." This interaction is a giveaway for the viewer but not for Truman.

In his cubicle, Truman is approached by his supervisor, Lawrence. Lawrence asks Truman to visit Welles Park, located on Harbor Island. Truman makes his way to the ferry dock and purchases a ticket. As he begins to cross the dock to the ferry, he becomes paralyzed. He stops and stares at a partially submerged dinghy beside the dock. At this point in the film, it has not been revealed that Truman's show father, Kirk, drowned in front of him as a child while sailing in a dinghy. The dinghy has clearly been placed there by Christof to remind Truman of the incident, which caused him to have aquaphobia. Before Truman turns around to go back to land, his eyes dart towards the bottom right of the frame. What is located in that space is something that was shown a moment earlier when Truman walked towards the terminal entrance, as well as through the blind of the ticket booth: a sailboat. Suffice it to say, this sailboat plays a critical role near the end of the film. Truman's darting eyes are extraordinary for foreshadowing how the film will end—and yet their status as such likely evades the viewer.

The Chef's Pal; Dreaming of Fiji; Memories of Dad

In the very next scene, something extraordinary is once again placed in front of the viewer. As Truman digs in his garden, a gnome wearing a similar hat and clothing to his can be seen sitting atop a globe. This garden piece tells the viewer not only how the film will end, namely, Truman will get outside of the "world" he lives in—it also tells the viewer where Truman will escape from, namely, a hole under the globe. Interestingly, when Meryl suddenly rides into the backyard area on her bike, Truman drops his shovel as if to hide what he was doing. Perhaps he had been checking the soil to see if a tunnel could be dug. When he sees that Meryl is not going to question him but rather show off the Chef's Pal she acquired at the supermarket, he picks the shovel back up and responds, with veiled sarcasm, "Wow! That's amazing!" Ironically, Truman will use the Chef's Pal to dig out of the basement.

While hitting golf balls off of a partially constructed bridge, Truman tells Marlon that he is contemplating leaving Seahaven. Marlon puts ice on the idea, claiming Truman has a great job. Truman then asks Marlon, "Don't you ever get antsy? Itchy feet?" This suggests that Truman wants to see more and know more. To diffuse the topic, Marlon asks, "Where is there to go?" Truman answers, "Fiji." He explains that Fiji is intriguing because "you can't get any farther away before you start coming back."[25] Later in the film, a flashback to Truman's time in college shows him being told that fellow student and love interest Sylvia is moving to Fiji. It follows that there is a dual motivation for Truman's contemplation of leaving Seahaven: a desire to see Sylvia and a desire to see more of the world. At this juncture, it is unclear which motivation is greater.

As Truman sits on the beach, he recalls—and the viewer is given a flashback to—the drowning of Kirk. When the flashback ends, a rain shower begins directly above Truman's head and follows him as he moves. Truman then raises his arms and makes the sound of a choir often used in television shows to indicate that a miracle has occurred. The event does seem to be "a transgression of a law of nature . . . by the interposition of some invisible agent," to employ David Hume's definition of a miracle.[26] Truman is somewhat aware of the extraordinary quality of the incident, yet he does not report it to Meryl or reflect on it further. The viewer once again scoffs at Truman's obliviousness to the extraordinary.

The viewer's frustration with Truman grows even greater when he bumps into the actor who played Kirk while walking to

25. Marlon says something to Truman right before the explanation, but there is no audio track present for his speech.

26. Hume, *Enquiry Concerning Human Understanding*, 127 [X.12.115].

work. The actor is grabbed by business people on the sidewalk and dragged into a transit bus; the doors close before Truman can enter. As in the scene with the lamp falling from the sky, but now even more absurdly, surrounding cast members do not react in any way to the ordeal. This time, Truman does report the incident to someone: his show mother, Angela. Unsurprisingly, Angela concocts an explanation, and she even goes so far as to imply that Truman is imagining his father alive because he feels guilty for playing a part in his death. The wicked side of the cast of The Truman Show comes into focus here. Later in the film, Meryl threatens Truman with the prospect of telling Angela about his behavior. It would seem Angela has played an intimidating role in Truman's life. In this scene, the film begins to replace comedy with tragedy, thus opening a door to the more serious subject of conversion.

"Lauren"; Paranoia; There's No Place Like Home

On his way to work, a public service message about driving safety begins skipping on Truman's car radio. Suddenly, the radio picks up communication between crew members. An announcer breaks in and lightheartedly remarks, "I guess we picked up a police frequency or something." The announcer goes on to deliver a safe driving message. At the end of the message there is, as earlier in the film, a question posed to Truman. This time, Truman does not answer. Instead, visibly frustrated, he turns the radio off. At this moment, Weir introduces Philip Glass's musical piece "Anthem Part II," which was originally used in the 1988 documentary film, *Powaqqatsi*. The word *powaqqatsi* is a Hopi neologism meaning "life in transition."

A close-up of a newspaper being held by a man is shown. The date of the newspaper is Friday, December 13. This could be another extraordinary item placed directly in front of the viewer. Friday, December 13 was the departure date of Francis Drake's circumnavigation of the earth, which involved taking possession of a boat named the *Santa Maria*.[27] If intentionally chosen by Weir, the newspaper date—like the darting eyes and garden gnome—informs the viewer of how *The Truman Show* will end. Indeed, Truman will take possession of a boat named the *Santa Maria* and head for a destination that has the prospect of circumnavigation: "You can't get any farther away before you start coming back."

Truman enters and immediately exits the revolving door at the front of his workplace. He sits down at an outdoor cafe table and scrutinizes his surroundings. He sees a man make eye contact then nervously look away. Truman grabs his briefcase off the table, runs towards the street, and a bus comes to a halt just inches from his face. Truman would have been killed were it not for Christof and his staff watching and directing traffic. What is distinct about this event is that Truman finally realizes there is something off about his world. Glass's "Anthem Part II" begins to play again. Truman decides to enter an office building that is not expecting him and briefly sees production crew behind a mock elevator.[28] Just as Truman's eyes widen, he is thrown out onto the street by security guards. The widening of eyes here is not only a passing physiological response to a surprising moment—it marks an expansion of Truman's attentiveness to his surroundings. On his exit, Truman hits a repairman with his briefcase and gets no reaction. Truman is testing his world, which opens the viewer to lessening his or her judgment of cognitive superiority over him. It will only be a minor lessening, however, since the inaction of the repairman is a dead giveaway for the viewer but not for Truman.

In the shot of Truman walking away from the office building, everyone is walking in slow motion except for him. It is not clear what Weir wants to convey through this shot, but at the very least, it frames Truman as less a member of the Seahaven population

27. Sugden, *Sir Francis Drake*, 103. In the Julian calendar, December 13, 1577 falls on a Friday.

28. The shot is similar to one in the 1960 *Twilight Zone* episode "People Are Alike All Over," where two panels slide open to reveal that the main character has been living in a cage with observers on the outside.

than before.[29] Truman sees Marlon at a nearby store and runs to him. He quietly remarks, "I'm on to something, Marlon. Something big." After this remark, Marlon stocks, unstocks, and restocks the vending machine. This escapes Truman's cognition but not the viewer's. Marlon responds, "This is one of your fantasies. I don't have time for that." Truman demands that they leave the store to talk further.

Truman and Marlon visit the beach to watch the sun set. Truman remarks, "Maybe I'm being set up for something. You ever think about that, Marlon—like your whole life has been building towards something?" This explicitly introduces a conversional tone to the film. Marlon thoughtlessly replies, "No." As they look at the sunset, Marlon says, "That's the big guy. Quite a paintbrush he's got," ironically referring to Christof. On this occasion, the suggestion of being fulfilled by Seahaven's beauty does not work. Truman remarks, "Just between you and me, Marlon, I'm going away for awhile."

Travelers Beware; Dented Beetle; "I'm Being Spontaneous!"

Truman makes a surprise visit to the hospital where Meryl supposedly works, followed by attempts to book a flight to Fiji and take a bus to Chicago. That Truman is still cognitively inattentive is shown by his failure to notice that the travel agent is wearing a makeup bib when she first sits down.

The ensuing scene marks the halfway point in the film. It is here that Truman begins to scrutinize extraordinary things, in this case a scripted cycle of people passing by his home: "lady, flowers, and there it is—there's the dented Beetle!" In response, Truman makes the same "miracle" sound that he did when rain followed him on the beach. This time, Truman does not let the incident go; he locks the doors to the car and informs Meryl that he is driving

---

29. Falzon examines Truman's challenging of social norms. See Falzon, "Peter Weir's *The Truman Show*," 18.

to Atlantic City. "Somebody help me, I'm being spontaneous!" he yells.

Blocked at Every Turn; Mococoa; Father and Son Reunion

Predictably, Truman's small side street becomes instantly gridlocked. Truman pretends to be returning home and suddenly veers in a different direction, now heading to New Orleans. Truman's spontaneity is rewarded, for he evades the gridlock and reaches the bridge that leaves Seahaven. After crossing the bridge, Truman is blocked by a feigned nuclear plant leak. A police officer stops Truman from advancing but accidentally calls him by name. As with the cycle of people near his home, Truman does not brush off the extraordinary event; rather, he is frightened and attempts to run away. Crew members dressed in hazmat suits quickly capture him.

Upon returning home, Truman questions Meryl's honesty after she performs an advertisement for Mococoa in front of him. He grabs Meryl and threatens her with the Chef's Pal. When Marlon barges in, Truman gives an expression akin to that of the figure in Edvard Munch's painting, *The Scream*.

In the scene that follows, Truman tells Marlon, "It feels like the whole world revolves around me somehow." He continues, "Everybody seems to be in on it." It is here, at the fifty-seven-minute mark of the film, that Christof reappears. Christof is shown feeding lines of dialogue to Marlon through an earpiece. Marlon tells Truman that he is not "in on it," and that he found someone for Truman: Kirk. "Go to him," Marlon says with no finesse. Truman's reaction to this extraordinary event does not match the viewer's cognitive inclination, namely, dismissal, but it is also not entirely naive. The way in which Truman utters "Dad!" is unenthusiastic, perhaps even feigned, which warrants some admiration from the viewer.

TruTalk; Do You Think He Knows?; "He's Gone."

As Bliss observes of Weir, there is a "riddle that he persistently poses: what do we really know, and how do we know what we know?"[30] At this juncture of the film, such questions, already posed discreetly, become plain. During TruTalk, Mike Michaelson asks Christof, "Why do you think that Truman has never come close to discovering the true nature of his world, until now?" Christof replies, "We accept the reality of the world with which we're presented. It's as simple as that." According to Weir, this line of dialogue is "a very concise way of stating the theme of the film."[31] After Christof delivers this critical line, Weir cuts to two parking garage attendants who unreflectively nod in agreement. The viewer is likely to snicker at the attendants' obliviousness, thinking they do not grasp the sense in which the line applies to them, but is the viewer not also guilty of treating reality in this way? The line reveals the character of Christof to be a conduit for Weir's conversional message. The line also reveals Christof to be benevolent in at least one way; if a viewer was to integrate the line of dialogue completely into his or her cognitive practice, he or she would not be shocked by the extraordinary thing near the end of the film. But Weir has been coaxing the viewer into feeling cognitively above Truman—and now the garage attendants—so that the extraordinary thing cannot but elicit conversion. Additional evidence of Christof's facilitation of Weir's message of conversion will appear shortly.

Sylvia calls in and asks Christof if he ever feels guilty. He replies, "Seahaven is the way the world should be." Christof sees Seahaven as the best of all possible worlds—a topic wrestled with by many philosophers. His statement attests to the sense in which he sees himself as all-good, and the viewer can at least agree that Christof has spared Truman the natural evils of pain and suffering. These are the phenomena that philosophers often point to as most difficult to reconcile with God's omnibenevolence. With these

30. Bliss, *Dreams within a Dream*, 25.
31. Kalina, "Designing Visions," 22.

removed from the scenario, the film engages the problem of evil solely in connection with Christof's deception of Truman. Sylvia focuses in on this point; she tells Christof, "He's not a performer; he's a prisoner." Christof responds,

> He could leave at any time. If his was more than just a vague ambition, if he was absolutely determined to discover the truth, there's no way we could prevent him. I think what distresses you, really, caller, is that ultimately, Truman prefers his cell, as you call it.

Christof turns the tables on Sylvia here by intimating that Truman's reluctance to challenge the illusion he has created essentially legitimates it.[32]

Truman retires to his basement after Meryl moves out; he appears to be asleep. This is not the case, however, as Truman sneaks to the closet and digs up to his garden using the Chef's Pal. One can see that the previously discussed gnome and globe have been moved to make room for the tunnel. The entire cast of The Truman Show angrily scours the streets of Seahaven looking for Truman. As Bliss points out, "the town's mask of good will [has fallen] off."[33] Truman's self-determination has brought out the real attitudes of the actors. Observing the search, Christof says, in a somewhat excited tone, "We need more light." This remark no doubt communicates a desire to catch Truman, but it can also be taken as a desire to achieve better filming conditions. "Cue the sun," Christof commands. Cast members are startled by the sudden transition, which shows that Christof is no longer giving them earpiece warnings.

---

32. While outside the focus of this chapter, there are intriguing aspects of the relationship between Sylvia and Christof. Both of them touch an image of Truman on a screen, and it is simply assumed that Christof's motivation is objectification and Sylvia's, love. Brief shots of her apartment walls suggest something more complicated: one can see a map of Seahaven, a list of cameras, non-professional photographs of cast members with captions such as "No hope, repeated tries," and the "You are on TV" sign worn by a person who parachuted into Seahaven.

33. Bliss, *Dreams within a Dream*, 173.

Setting Sail; Cue the Storm; The Sky's the Limit

Christof finally spots Truman in a sailboat, the *Santa Maria*, on one of the control room monitors. That this sailboat is the same one Truman's eyes darted towards early in the film is confirmed by its absence in a brief scene at the terminal. Christof delays telling crew members, reaffirming the close connection he has with Truman. An executive asks, "How do we stop him?" Christof makes eye contact with Simeon, who then reluctantly announces, "We're going to be accessing the weather program now." There is a shot here of a computer screen, and it shows that the *Santa Maria* contains more than twenty cameras. This marks yet another extraordinary thing placed in plain sight of the viewer. The film has made it clear that cameras are always on Truman, and that Truman is terrified of water, so the presence of even one camera on the sailboat is extraordinary, let alone more than twenty.[34] It seems Christof placed a camera-filled sailboat at the ferry terminal for Truman to notice, anticipating that he would one day decide to escape. Strictly speaking, then, Christof creates the conditions for Truman's conversion—and for Weir's conversional message to us.

A storm begins around Truman's sailboat. As Truman frantically tries to stay aboard, Christof demands, "Give me some lightning. Again. Hit him again!" After falling into the water, Truman successfully gets back into the sailboat. Christof walks away from the crew, looks downward at Truman from the control room window, and discreetly nods his head. Christof seems impressed by Truman's determination, now cognizant that he is going to put up a fight. Truman tauntingly yells, "Is that the best you can do? You're going to have to kill me!" It seems Truman's motivation for leaving Seahaven has become purely intellectual, for dying on the way to meet Sylvia would naturally exclude the possibility of ever reconnecting with her. Christof demands, "Capsize him. Tip him over." Simeon declines, so Christof pushes the button himself,

---

34. In the shooting script, Niccol states that the *Santa Maria* circled and filmed Kirk drowning in front of Truman. Unsurprisingly, there is no indication of this in the film; twenty cameras would not be required to film Kirk drowning from a distance.

showing a slight smile. When Truman nearly drowns, Christof quietly says, "That's enough." He then bows his head, almost in the manner of having completed a mission. It seems Christof went as far as he needed in order to test whether Truman was "absolutely determined to discover the truth," as he put it during TruTalk. Truman climbs back into the boat and begins sailing again.

What has been referred to above as the extraordinary thing near the end of the film now comes to pass. This is the moment of conversion, for Truman and, potentially, the viewer. With only the slightest visual warning in the form of a shadow, the bowsprit of Truman's sailboat loudly breaks through the edge of the dome, which is painted like a sky. Simone Knox describes it as a "fake horizon."[35] As Bliss points out, the viewer and Truman are equally shocked by the event.[36] What was taken as real is not, and what was taken as real could not be any more extensive: the entire sky. Cognitive superiority over Truman will, for converted viewers, change to equality as a result of the event. Moreover, such viewers will now stand in admiration of Truman's determination to discover the truth, having seen how easy it is to fail to adequately grasp what is right in front of oneself. Weir has been planting seeds for this lesson from the beginning, with Truman's darting eyes, the garden gnome, (potentially) the newspaper date, and filling a sailboat with cameras. Each of these items, which happen *to* the viewer of the film, are just as extraordinary as the various events that happen *to* Truman; the difference is that now, Truman and the viewer experience the same extraordinary event—and on the same level. However, as noted above, only some viewers will grasp the implication of the bowsprit event for themselves; those who do not grasp it will be given one more chance in the final shot of the film.

Truman reaches out, touches the sky with his hand, and exhales. Touching the sky, according to Weir, "[is] a classically archetypal Jungian image."[37] Carl Jung held that our ancient ancestors

35. Knox, "Reading *The Truman Show*," 13.

36. Bliss, *Dreams within a Dream*, 180.

37. Danielsen, "Back on the A-list," 6, quoted in Leonard, "Mystical Gaze," 56–57.

associated the sky with transcendence.[38] To say that Truman touches transcendence is to verify Leonard's claim that in Weir's films, a relationship with a metaphysical world comes to be taken seriously. Weir is, in the deepest way, prompting the viewer to go beyond a thoughtless acceptance of a world just there—an attitude that accompanies rudimentary forms of materialism.

Truman first exhibits relief at having discovered the truth about Seahaven. However, he soon begins to hit the sky with his hand, followed by his elbow. These actions express his anger not only at having been deceived but also at having subscribed to an incorrect world view. Weir consciously chose to film this from Truman's back so he could have privacy in this life-changing moment.[39] The viewer who grasps the personal implications of this joins Truman, now so closely involved with his ordeal as to feel alone with him. In short, the shot of Truman's back provides the nearest analogue of reading while alone that is possible within the environment of a movie theater.

Truman spots a staircase and makes his way to it, walking along the edge of the dome. The staircase leads to a door marked "Exit." He ascends the stairs, again touching the sky with his hand.

"Who Am I?"; Good Afternoon, Good Evening, and Good Night; Credits

Truman pushes the exit door open. Christof comes on a loud speaker and says, "Truman, you can speak. I can hear you." Truman turns around and asks, "Who are you?" Christof states that he is the creator of a television show in which Truman is the star. Truman asks, "Was nothing real?" It is worth reproducing Christof's reply in full:

> You were real. That's what made you so good to watch. Listen to me, Truman. There's no more truth out there than there is in the world I created for you. The same lies.

38. Lewis, *Astrology Book*, 163.

39. "The Making of *The Truman Show*, Part II," contained on the DVD.

> The same deceit. But in my world, you have nothing to
> fear. I know you better than you know yourself.

Truman interrupts Christof, stating that there was no camera in
his head. Kimberly Blessing finds in this statement an echo of the
Meditations, for the malicious demon "can never make [Descartes]
doubt his existence as a thinking thing."[40] Christof disregards Truman's statement and continues:

> You're afraid. That's why you can't leave. It's okay, Tru-
> man. I understand. I have been watching you your whole
> life. I was watching when you were born. I was watching
> when you took your first step. I watched you on your first
> day of school. The episode when you lost your first tooth.
> You can't leave, Truman. You belong here, with me. Talk
> to me. Say something. Well, say something [expletive].
> You're on television. You're live to the whole world.

Truman smiles and says, "In case I don't see you, good afternoon,
good evening, and goodnight." He then tilts his head, laughs deri-
sively, and utters a mysterious "Yeah!" that he has employed at several points in the film. After taking a bow, he steps through the exit
door. Bliss writes, "[Truman] steps completely outside the realm
of what has formerly passed for reality."[41] This is where Truman
starts over. The fact of starting over is attested to by the complete
darkness of the door. The senses offer Truman no preview of where
he is going—and no hint of whether it will resemble "the world
with which he has been presented," to use Christof's words from
TruTalk.[42] The fact that Truman places his foot on a surface inside
the door should not be taken as nullifying an additional statement
about materialism. Failing to show Truman stepping onto something and moving forward would leave the viewer uncertain that
he went through with leaving Seahaven. If one brackets the filmic
requirement of a surface inside the door, Truman stepping through

---

40. Blessing, "Deceit and Doubt," 6.

41. Bliss, *Dreams within a Dream*, 171.

42. Sylvia would be an exception were it not for her show father telling
Truman that she has psychotic episodes; even she remains an uncertainty for
Truman as he steps through the door.

represents an abandonment of materialism. Stepping through the door means dropping all expectations, including materialism's expectation that whatever one encounters is fundamentally material.

In the final shot of the film, one parking garage attendant asks, "What else is on?" and his coworker replies, "Yeah, let's see what else is on." Viewers into whom Truman's conversion has yet to be induced are likely to sneer at the ignorance of the attendants, only to be immediately jolted by Weir's recommencement of the uneasy music used during Christof's storm at sea. This music suggests one final time that the film is a conversion work. Weir wants the film to keep making itself in the viewer's head, not just in the sense of imagining a denouement but in the sense of continuing Truman's story in one's own life. Viewers into whom conversion has been induced step through the exit door of the movie theater with a commitment to start over—to not simply accept the reality of the world with which they are presented.

5

Conversion Works, Ernest Becker's *The Denial of Death*, and Education

Preliminary Remarks

THIS BOOK HAS SHOWN that Augustine of Hippo's *Confessions*, René Descartes's *Meditations on First Philosophy*, Bernard Lonergan's *Insight: A Study of Human Understanding*, and Peter Weir's *The Truman Show* contain and induce conversion. Conversion, to reiterate, means abandoning a world view and starting over.[1] The book has also shown that cognitive imitation and private engagement play a role in all four works. To reiterate, cognitive imitation means replicating the mental activities of the individual who undergoes conversion in the work, and private engagement means reading or viewing the work while alone. Works containing all four features above were deemed to belong to a class named conversion works.

This chapter argues for the contemporary educational value of conversion works—certainly the four works considered but potentially others. The argument involves an extensive engagement with cultural anthropologist Ernest Becker's *The Denial of Death*,

---

1. This definition is adapted from MacDonald, "Philosophical Conversion," 304.

published in 1973.[2] The first section of this chapter provides an overview of this work. For the first half of the overview, it will appear as though *The Denial of Death* is disconnected from the four works. However, in the second half of the overview, striking implications for them come into focus—especially via Becker's concept of immortality-vehicles. The second section of this chapter outlines these implications and takes them to attest in a general way to the contemporary educational value of the works. The third and final section makes more particular and practical educational remarks about the works.

Overview of Ernest Becker's *The Denial of Death*

Becker obtained a PhD in cultural anthropology at Syracuse University in 1960 and went on to teach at institutions in the United States and Canada.[3] He authored nine books over the course of his life. *The Denial of Death* earned him a Pulitzer Prize.

Becker begins with an examination of heroism. He contends that "our central calling, our main task on this planet, is the heroic."[4] To be a hero, in Becker's view, is simply to stand out in some respect. Now, a human being always-already stands out among other life-forms by virtue of his or her self-consciousness. There is a kind of baseline self-esteem that is afforded solely by the uniqueness of being human. Coupled with this baseline self-esteem is an inescapable narcissism, for one also possesses a completely unique "face and name."[5] One is number one in one's own mind, ready to "recreate the whole world out of ourselves even if no one else

---

2. Readers might also consult Becker's earlier but education-focused reflections in *Beyond Alienation*. This work is somewhat difficult to obtain. More easily accessed is Becker, "Theory of Alienation"—an informative excerpt from the work.

3. Additional background can be found in Sally Kenel's concise biography of Becker. See Kenel, *Mortal Gods*, 9–27.

4. Becker, *Denial of Death*, 1.

5. Becker, *Denial of Death*, 69.

existed."[6] The first threat to our self-esteem, Becker explains, is the birth of a sibling who also sees him or herself as number one. The category "second best" appears the moment one's sibling is given a bigger piece of candy.[7]

What Becker offers above is not, despite appearances, an indictment of human beings. Rather, he is describing a tragic situation. He explains,

> [I]t is not that children are vicious, selfish, or domineering. It is that they so openly express man's tragic destiny: he must desperately justify himself as an object of primary value in the universe; he must stand out, be a hero, make the biggest possible contribution to world life, show that he *counts* more than anything or anyone else.[8]

The urge to be a hero is something that few adults are likely to admit because of its intertwinement with narcissism. There exists a "terror of admitting what one is doing to earn his self-esteem."[9] Consequently, adults satiate the urge with pursuits that are less obviously heroic. The forms of concealed heroism are vast and vary from culture to culture. Becker explains,

> It doesn't matter whether the cultural hero-system is frankly magical, religious, and primitive or secular, scientific, and civilized. It is still a mythical hero-system in which people serve in order to earn a feeling of primary value, of cosmic specialness, of ultimate usefulness to creation, of unshakable meaning. They earn this feeling by carving out a place in nature, by building an edifice that reflects human value: a temple, a cathedral, a totem pole, a skyscraper, a family that spans three generations. The hope and belief is that the things that man creates in society are of lasting worth and meaning, that they

---

6. Becker, *Denial of Death*, 2.
7. Becker, *Denial of Death*, 3.
8. Becker, *Denial of Death*, 4. Italics in the original.
9. Becker, *Denial of Death*, 6.

outlive or outshine death and decay, that man and his products count.[10]

Becker contends that there is a modern-day "crisis of heroism"[11] because of "the disappearance of convincing dramas of heroic apotheosis of man."[12] It is not only religious hero-systems that are found to be unconvincing but increasingly the secular alternatives of communism, scientism, and consumerism.[13]

Becker goes on to state that "heroism is first and foremost a reflex of the terror of death."[14] The terror or fear of death is therefore more basic than the urge to be a hero and in need of closer analysis. Against the environmental view of the genesis of the fear of death, which sees it as resulting from a depriving mother, Becker claims it is biologically innate. He concurs with psychoanalyst Gregory Zilboorg that the fear of death is "an expression of the instinct of self-preservation, which functions as a constant drive to maintain life and to master the dangers that threaten life."[15] It is here that the meaning of the title, *The Denial of Death*, becomes clear. Becker writes,

> [T]he fear of death must be present behind all our nor-
> mal functioning, in order for the organism to be armed
> toward self-preservation. But the fear of death cannot be
> present constantly in one's mental functioning, else the
> organism could not function.[16]

It would be debilitating to constantly think about one's impending death, thus one's consciousness of it is repressed. However, like most repressions, it still influences one's behavior. One continually fights against one's impending death, even if one refuses to admit it. There is a double denial taking place here: denying death in

10. Becker, *Denial of Death*, 5.
11. Becker, *Denial of Death*, 6.
12. Becker, *Denial of Death*, 190.
13. Becker, *Denial of Death*, 7.
14. Becker, *Denial of Death*, 11.
15. Becker, *Denial of Death*, 16.
16. Becker, *Denial of Death*, 16.

one's behavior and denying that one is denying death in one's behavior. Disconcertingly, Becker writes, "[O]ne's whole life is a style or a scenario with which one tries to deny oblivion and to extend oneself beyond death in symbolic ways."[17] Becker gives several examples of such self-extension, and they range far beyond believing in an afterlife. He includes constructing a monument, writing a book, winning a war, and spearheading an intellectual movement. Each of these is to some extent an "immortality-vehicle."[18]

Becker goes on to bring the topic of the fear of death into contact with philosophy. He states that philosophers never found the essence of the human being—"something fixed in his nature, deep down, some special quality or substance"—because "the essence of man is really his *paradoxical* nature, the fact that he is half animal and half symbolic."[19] It is important to be clear on the anthropology that Becker introduces here, for it radiates throughout *The Denial of Death*. He writes,

> The person is both a self and a body, and from the beginning there is the confusion about where "he" really "is"—in the symbolic inner self or in the physical body. Each phenomenological realm is different. The inner self represents the freedom of thought, imagination, and the infinite reach of symbolism. The body represents determinism and boundness.[20]

Human nature is paradoxical because the body and the self "can never be reconciled seamlessly."[21] The human being is pulled in two directions, as it were, and his or her awareness of this fact is what makes the human predicament especially tragic. Becker writes,

> [M]an is a union of opposites, of self-consciousness and of physical body. Man emerged from the instinctive

---

17. Becker, *Denial of Death*, 104.
18. Becker, *Denial of Death*, 110.
19. Becker, *Denial of Death*, 25–26. Italics in the original.
20. Becker, *Denial of Death*, 41–42.
21. Becker, *Denial of Death*, 29.

thoughtless action of the lower animals and came to reflect on his condition. He was given a consciousness of his individuality and his part-divinity in creation, the beauty and uniqueness of his face and name. At the same time he was given the consciousness of the terror of the world and of his own death and decay. This paradox is the really constant thing about man in all periods of history and society; it is thus the true "essence" of man, as [Erich] Fromm said.[22]

Human beings reside between animals and angels—and the ambiguities of this condition are what cause anxiety. Becker explains,

[A]nxiety . . . results from the human paradox that man is an animal who is conscious of his animal limitation. Anxiety is the result of the perception of the truth of one's condition. What does it mean to be a *self-conscious animal*? The idea is ludicrous, if it is not monstrous. It means to know that one is food for worms.[23]

It is crucial to note that Becker subsumes under "animal limitation" both being subject to death and to bodily functions. Regarding the former, Becker notes that an animal can stand idly while the animal next to it is killed because there is no knowledge of death until it happens. Human beings, by contrast, have full knowledge that death is impending. Repressing knowledge of one's impending death, and of one's animal characteristics, is inevitable in Becker's view since "a full apprehension of man's condition would drive him insane."[24]

The most consistent or stretched out form of denying one's condition is one's "life style."[25] Becker refers to one's life style as "a vital lie," "a *necessary* and basic dishonesty about oneself and

---

22. Becker, *Denial of Death*, 68–69.

23. Becker, *Denial of Death*, 87. Italics in the original.

24. Becker, *Denial of Death*, 27. Later he adds, "Man must always imagine and believe in a 'second' reality or a better world than the one that is given him by nature." Becker, *Denial of Death*, 188.

25. Becker, *Denial of Death*, 55.

one's whole situation."[26] The dishonesty being referred to pertains to uncontrollable aspects of creatureliness, as well as one's uncontrollable dependence on things external to oneself: "a god," "a stronger person," "the power of an all-absorbing activity, a passion, a dedication to a game."[27] Each of these maintains equanimity—that is, mental stability—and shields one from the danger of possibility.

Drawing on philosopher Søren Kierkegaard, Becker outlines some "styles of denying possibility, or the lies of character—which is the same thing."[28] In one style, the human being is "lulled by the daily routines of his society, content with the satisfactions that it offers him: . . . the car, the shopping center, the two-week summer vacation."[29] These are "purely external men, playing successfully the standardized hero-game into which we happen to fall by accident, by family connection, by reflex patriotism," and so on.[30] Such persons are "'inauthentic' in that they do not belong to themselves."[31] Another style is found in the person "who tries to cultivate his interiority"[32] and is "content to toy—in his periodic solitudes—with the idea of who he might really be."[33] These introspective persons appear to be facing their true condition, and thus appear authentic, but they are not. Despite carrying out self-reflection these persons have not arrived at genuine self-knowledge, for the attainment of it would be marked by a loss, rather than gain, of equanimity.

26. Becker, *Denial of Death*, 55. Italics in the original.

27. Becker, *Denial of Death*, 55.

28. Becker, *Denial of Death*, 73.

29. Becker, *Denial of Death*, 74.

30. Becker, *Denial of Death*, 82–83. He elaborates, "As soon as a man lifts his nose from the ground and starts sniffing at eternal problems like life and death, the meaning of a rose or a star cluster—then he is in trouble." Becker, *Denial of Death*, 178.

31. Becker, *Denial of Death*, 73.

32. Becker, *Denial of Death*, 82.

33. Becker, *Denial of Death*, 83.

With so much talk of the tragedy of the human predicament, one begins to wonder if there is any solution whatsoever. It is precisely at this moment that Becker offers a remedial path. He writes,

> The "healthy" person, the true individual, the self-realized soul, the "real" man, is the one who has *transcended* himself. How does one transcend himself; how does he open himself to new possibility? By realizing the truth of his situation, by dispelling the lie of his character, by breaking his spirit out of its conditioned prison.[34]

To be clear, dispelling the lie of character means giving up the traits or beliefs that are affording one equanimity. To carry this out is to discover one's "'authentic self': what we really are without sham, without disguise, without defenses against fear."[35] Suddenly, one stands unprotected, but also—and for the first time—open to possibility. Becker elaborates,

> And so the arrival at new possibility, at new reality, by the destruction of the self through facing up to the anxiety of the terror of existence. The self must be destroyed, brought down to nothing, in order for self-transcendence to begin. Then the self can begin to relate itself to powers beyond itself.[36]

In this process of beginning again, the self is not removed but rather pared down to the point where a "relationship to the Ultimate Power, to infinitude" becomes possible.[37] These terms are carefully chosen, for Becker does not wish to speak of the divine with specificity. This approach carries over into his view of faith. Faith is something that an authentic person must adopt in order to bear the burden of standing unprotected. It is

> the faith that one's very creatureliness has some meaning to a Creator; that despite one's true insignificance, weakness, death, one's existence has meaning in some

34. Becker, *Denial of Death*, 86. Indentation removed.
35. Becker, *Denial of Death*, 57.
36. Becker, *Denial of Death*, 89.
37. Becker, *Denial of Death*, 90.

ultimate sense because it exists within an eternal and infinite scheme of things brought about and maintained to some kind of design by some creative force.[38]

Faith is thus a kind of basic trust in the face of futility. Faith does not fully overcome the anxiety that comes with being authentic—it allows one to creatively manage anxiety. Facing up to anxiety through faith serves as "an eternal spring for growth into new dimensions of thought and trust,"[39] and as a means of curtailing one's manipulation of others.[40]

Implications for the Four Works

Although the general phrase "the four works" is used in what follows, the analysis principally applies to the portion of the works that have received examination in this book: Book VII of the *Confessions*, the First and Second Meditation in the *Meditations*, chapters 1 to 11 of *Insight*, and the entirety of *The Truman Show*.

The relevance of *The Denial of Death* to the four works seems straightforward at first glance. All four works feature the abandonment of the very overarching conception of reality that prohibits the immortality of the soul: materialism. There is at play, then, at least some struggle—conscious or unconscious—against impending death.[41] It is in Becker's concept of immortality-vehicles, however, that one finds the deeper implications of *The Denial of Death* for the four works. Of the examples of immortality-vehicles that Becker provides, two are especially relevant: writing a book and

38. Becker, *Denial of Death*, 90.

39. Becker, *Denial of Death*, 92.

40. Becker, *Denial of Death*, 258.

41. While this book explores conversion as a non-religious phenomenon, there are, of course, important links between human motivation, religion, and mortality. A springboard for exploring this matter may be found in Donald Wiebe's reflections on the topic. Wiebe remarks, "The recognition of human limitation—of finitude—in the face of the inexorable processes of nature that eventuate in death, and the transcending of those limitations is what religion is essentially all about." Wiebe, *Irony of Theology*, 33.

spearheading an intellectual movement. These must be taken up at length.

A book is an immortality-vehicle insofar as the self of the author is extended beyond death in it in a symbolic way. More than having a child, a book allows an author "[to] feel that he is truly perpetuating his own inner self, his distinctive personality, his spirit, as it were."[42] This is especially true of autobiographies. The case would seem to be closed, then, for the *Confessions*, *Meditations*, and *Insight*—all of them autobiographical in character. However, there are two features of these works that mitigate the charge. First, the goal of inducing conversion puts instructional concerns above self-extension in the text. It is Augustine the narrator, Descartes the narrator, and an ideal version of Lonergan who undergo conversion, not the authors themselves. In short, their true self or true personality is not perpetuated in the works considered. It goes without saying that this point applies maximally to *The Truman Show*, where a fictional character with no connection to Weir undergoes conversion. The present vein of analysis does not apply to the film.

The second mitigating factor initially seems to be a magnifying factor: cognitive imitation. Inasmuch as all three written works beckon their engager to adopt the thinking employed in them, it would seem that a replica of the author's thought—shaped for instruction as it is—is left not only on the page but also in the reader's mind. It is only through a closer look at how cognitive imitation operates that the non-extension of such imitation comes to light. In all three works, cognitive imitation unfolds gradually, and it entails the provision of accessible examples: sunlight, the elephant, and the sparrow in the *Confessions*; the piece of wax or the figures with hats and coats in the *Meditations*; the definition of a circle (or the constructed example of a game show) in *Insight*.[43]

42. Becker, *Denial of Death*, 231.

43. It is worth acknowledging the irony of the power that these banal examples had not only in their own time but in the centuries that followed. In fact, scenarios similar to Descartes's hats-and-coats example have been invoked by several contemporary philosophers in dealing with what is referred to as the Gettier problem. For instance, Roderick Chisholm describes a man

All of these allow the engager to slowly and personally experience the cognitive development that the author deems necessary to proceed. Through this process, the reader's native cognitive tools are illuminated; it is a matter of discovery, rather than manipulation. Those who do not discover the tools within themselves do not, and for the authors, should not, move forward. It is this respect for the possibility of withdrawing from the text—and from the offer of conversion—that further mitigates a charge of symbolic self-extension.

An additional question regarding cognitive imitation remains to be asked. Recall Becker's distinction between "purely external" individuals who play "the standardized hero-game into which [they] happen to fall by accident" and those who "cultivate [their] interiority" by means of "periodic solitudes." If one were to stop here, it would be plain that the authors of the three written works fall into the latter category. However, Becker asserts a further characteristic of that group: they gain equanimity through their interiority, which renders them inauthentic. Now, we do not have immediate access to the minds of the three authors to measure this definitively, but we can assess what is on display in the individuals who have a conversion in their works. Augustine the narrator opens Book VII by describing himself as "a man with profound defects,"[44] and his striving for conversion is coupled with "groaning" and "crashing."[45] Descartes the narrator opens the First Meditation with troubling uncertainty, and he closes it in a state of "inextricable darkness."[46] The idealized Lonergan speaks of a "startling strangeness."[47] Each of these exudes a loss, rather than gain, of equanimity. This opens up candidacy for the category

---

who believes that a sheep is in a field, but what he is looking at is actually a dog; however, in another part of the field, there is a sheep. Chisholm goes on to discuss whether or not it can be said that the man "knows" there is a sheep in the field. See Chisholm, *Theory of Knowledge*, 93.

44. Augustine, *Confessions*, 7.1.1.

45. Augustine, *Confessions*, 7.17.23. Becker himself mentions Augustine's self-awareness in this domain. See Becker, *Denial of Death*, 55–56.

46. Descartes, *Meditations*, 2:15 [23].

47. Lonergan, *Insight*, 22.

beyond the inauthentic external and internal ones; it is the category Becker describes above as "the true individual, the self-realized soul, . . . the one who has *transcended* himself." Before tackling that candidacy, however, the other example of an immortality-vehicle that Becker offers must be discussed.

Becker describes the psychoanalytic movement, which was spearheaded by Sigmund Freud, as an immortality-vehicle.[48] Specifically, Becker sees Freud as desiring to extend his genius beyond death through the movement.[49] The attribution of conscious desire is not surprising given the scale of an intellectual movement. That is, where one could legitimately question whether an author is conscious of his or her book as an immortality-vehicle, an intellectual who launches a movement must be aware, to some degree, of the self-extension involved.

When the above is brought to bear on the three written works considered, a question of relevance immediately arises. Indeed, the *Confessions* launches a form of Neoplatonism, the *Meditations* a form of dualism, and *Insight* a form of critical realism.[50] But already the qualifier "a form of" puts some distance between the creators and Becker's focus on spearheading, and even more distance is established by something this book highlights in the three works: starting over. The reason this book said little about the –isms listed above is that the implications of the adoption of those –isms are found in the portions of the works that ensue conversion. It is only after Book VII, after the Second Meditation, and after chapter 11 of the works that the structure and contents of reality are proposed in detail. When the authors commence this activity of starting over, the reader is free to do the same without their influence. This is a completely unique feature of conversion works, and it is the basis for judging that whatever intellectual

48. Becker, *Denial of Death*, 110.

49. Becker, *Denial of Death*, 110.

50. To reiterate a point from chapter 4, this book refrains from speculating about the –ism, if any, that *The Truman Show* suggests as a replacement for materialism.

movements have or might flow out of the post-conversion portion of the works, the presence of self-extension therein is dampened. Another factor in the consideration of intellectual movements was noted in this book's Introduction. In all four works, starting over is accompanied by the minimization or removal of the expectations of cognitive imitation and private engagement. In the *Confessions*, both expectations are removed from Book X onward. In the *Meditations*, both expectations are minimized from the Third Meditation onward. In *Insight*, cognitive imitation is removed and private engagement is minimized from chapter 12 onward. In *The Truman Show*, both expectations are removed just as the film ends, thus it once again stands outside the analysis. In terms of the three written works, the altering of cognitive imitation at the juncture in which the authors begin to systematically address the structure and contents of reality means that the reader possesses all the tools necessary to assess the world view about to be proposed. The adjustment of private engagement frees the reader to discuss the forms of –isms proposed in the post-conversion portion of the works if desired.

All of the above anticipates but does not confirm that the converted individual in each work is worthy of Becker's third category, namely, "the one who has *transcended* himself." As it happens, the category brings *The Truman Show* back into the discussion. Recall that for Becker, the self must be "brought down to nothing . . . in order for self-transcendence to begin." The effect of doing so is "the arrival at new possibility, at new reality." The question, then, is whether Augustine the narrator, Descartes the narrator, the ideal version of Lonergan, and Truman self-transcend and open up new possibility. The answer, with minor caveats, is yes. It is not a coincidence that these two markers are most visible in the most recently produced work considered: *The Truman Show*. Released in 1998, Weir's film captures the fragility of selfhood more intensely than any of the other works. As Truman sets sail near the end of the film, he gives up the exhaustive assurance and peace of mind that Seahaven has afforded him. As he steps through the dome's exit door, he enters a new reality that offers no promises. Out of all four works, only Truman's decision to start over approximates what Becker refers to as faith. Truman stands completely unprotected, to use Becker's term, but also completely open to possibility.

Descartes the narrator, the ideal version of Lonergan, and Augustine the narrator—in that decreasing order of intensity— also exhibit a paring down of the self. Descartes rids his mind "of all worries" and scrutinizes what he "originally believed [himself] to be."[51] Lonergan searches deeper than the moments when "the self . . . functions . . . as a self-attached and self-interested center within its own narrow world of stimuli and responses" to isolate "the same self as inquiring and reflecting, as conceiving intelligently and judging reasonably, . . . confronted with a universe of being."[52] Augustine realizes that he has "no clear vision . . . of [his] own self"[53] and laments his "customary condition."[54] All of these statements at least approach what Becker names self-transcendence,[55] and although the acts of starting over in the three works are not as radically open to possibility as Truman's act, they do permit a new overarching conception of reality.

It is hoped that the four works have been shown to elude the perils that Becker identifies. Surviving Becker's cautions already confers educational value onto the works. Nonetheless, it is prudent to offer some more particular and practical educational remarks—remarks informed by the engagement of *The Denial of Death* carried out above.

Education

The preceding chapters of this book isolated the plot points in four arcs of conversion. As noted in the Introduction, plotting these points, and reproducing the reflections of various scholars on

51. Descartes, *Meditations*, 2:17 [25].

52. Lonergan, *Insight*, 498.

53. Augustine, *Confessions*, 7.1.2.

54. Augustine, *Confessions*, 7.17.23.

55. It is worth mentioning here Glenn Hughes's critical analysis of Becker's notion of self-transcendence. See Hughes, *Transcendence and History*, 210.

them, serves educators who might teach one or more of the works. Needless to say, this book primarily serves educators in teaching the portions of the works that contain those arcs: Book VII of the *Confessions*, the First and Second Meditation in the *Meditations*, chapters 1 to 11 of *Insight*, and the entirety of *The Truman Show*. In our fast-paced world, full of distractions as it is, an increasing number of educators are likely to assign only portions of works. This might constitute a loss in some cases, but not with the three written works, given the self-contained learning experiences available in the portions examined. As has been stressed above and throughout, the examined portions of the three written works provide all of the tools necessary for (potentially) having the same conversion as the individual in the work. In addition, the works' expectation of private engagement, which an educator might draw attention to in assigning these portions, sharpens the attention given to them by a learner.

It is important to stress that the arcs of conversion are of a reasonable length to be engaged between being assigned and being discussed in a communal setting.[56] Private engagement of an entire arc allows the learner to join the individual in the work and independently react to the offer of conversion—that is, without coercion by the educator. Of course, it is only realistic to expect some learners to require assistance understanding one or more of the plot points in the arc of conversion. This very book has appealed to an array of scholarly reflections on the works in order to isolate and elaborate on these plot points. Such learners would benefit from assistance that is informed by the cautions that Becker advances. Another category of learner is the one who is ambivalent to the offer of conversion, even after assistance. This scenario should not be interpreted as a loss, for the learner has still undergone a degree of conceptual refinement by traversing the path traveled by the individual who has a conversion. In ordinary persuasive works of philosophy, engagement is considered worthwhile only if one accepts the conclusion of the argument that has been made. Conversion works, by contrast, yield educational benefits even to learners who

---

56. If necessary, learners can pass over chapters 2 to 5 of *Insight*.

ultimately decline the offer of conversion. As the Introduction to this book explained, the general term conversion was selected to appreciate an assortment of results from engaging the works.

What can also be safely assumed about learners today, in addition to regular distraction, is a heightened sensitivity to manipulation. Recall that chapters 1 to 3 of this book began with a brief biography. The biographies ceased at the juncture in which the target work was published, relaying only those elements of the creators' lives that inform it. Educators may wish to sum up a given biography for learners prior to assigning a work. The purpose of sharing these details is to alert the learner that what they are about to engage stems from real persons confronting concrete situations. Awareness of the autobiographical rootedness of the three works allays concerns about malicious intent. While indeed seeking to convert, the three written works are fundamentally driven by a desire to share, rather than force, a conversion.

Bibliography

Augustine of Hippo. *Confessions.* Translated by Henry Chadwick. Oxford: Oxford University Press, 1991.

Beck, L. J. *The Metaphysics of Descartes: A Study of the "Meditations."* Oxford: Clarendon, 1965.

Becker, Ernest. *Beyond Alienation: A Philosophy of Education for the Crisis of Democracy.* New York: George Braziller, 1967.

————. *The Denial of Death.* New York: Free, 1973.

————. "A Theory of Alienation as a Philosophy of Education." In *The Ernest Becker Reader,* edited by Daniel Liechty, 105–20. Seattle: University of Washington Press, 2005.

Blessing, Kimberly A. "Deceit and Doubt: The Search for Truth in *The Truman Show* and Descartes's *Meditations.*" In *Movies and the Meaning of Life: Philosophers Take on Hollywood,* edited by Kimberly A. Blessing and Paul J. Tudico, 3–16. Peru, IL: Open Court, 2005.

Bliss, Michael. *Dreams within a Dream: The Films of Peter Weir.* Carbondale, IL: Southern Illinois University Press, 2000.

————. "Keeping a Sense of Wonder: Interview with Peter Weir." *Film Quarterly* 53, no. 1 (1999) 2–11.

Broughton, Janet. *Descartes's Method of Doubt.* Princeton, NJ: Princeton University Press, 2002.

Brown, Peter. *Augustine of Hippo: A Biography.* New ed. Berkeley: University of California Press, 2000.

Budenholzer, Frank E. "Emergence, Probability, and Reductionism." *Zygon* 39, no. 2 (2004) 339–56.

Byrne, Patrick H. "Statistics as Science: Lonergan, McShane, and Popper." *Journal of Macrodynamic Analysis* 3 (2003) 55–75.

Cary, Phillip. *Augustine's Invention of the Inner Self: The Legacy of a Christian Platonist.* New York: Oxford University Press, 2000.

Chadwick, Henry. *Augustine: A Very Short Introduction.* New ed. New York: Oxford University Press, 2001.

———. *Heresy and Orthodoxy in the Early Church*. Aldershot, UK: Variorum, 1991.

———. Introduction to *Confessions*, by Augustine of Hippo, ix–xxvi. Translated by Henry Chadwick. Oxford: Oxford University Press, 1991.

Chisholm, Roderick. *Theory of Knowledge*. 3rd ed. Englewood Cliffs, NJ: Prentice Hall, 1989.

Clarke, Desmond M. *Descartes: A Biography*. New York: Cambridge University Press, 2006.

Conant, James. "An Interview with Stanley Cavell." In *The Senses of Stanley Cavell*, edited by Richard Fleming and Michael Payne, 21–72. Lewisburg, PA: Bucknell University Press, 1989.

Coyle, J. Kevin. *Manichaeism and its Legacy*. Boston: Brill, 2009.

Curley, Edwin. "Descartes, René." In *Encyclopedia of Philosophy*, 2nd ed., edited by Donald M. Borchert, 2:720–56. Detroit: Macmillan, 2006.

Descartes, René. *The Philosophical Writings of Descartes*. 3 vols. Translated by John Cottingham, et al. New York: Cambridge University Press, 1984–1991. *Discourse on the Method* is found in 1:111–51. *Meditations on First Philosophy* is found in 2:1–397. Personal letter with the heading "To Mersenne, 8 January 1641" is found in 3:171–3.

Drozdek, Adam. *Greek Philosophers as Theologians: The Divine* Arche. Aldershot, UK: Ashgate, 2007.

Dupont, Anthony, and Mateusz Stróżyński. "Augustine's Ostia Revisited: A Plotinian or Christian Ascent in Confessiones 9?" *International Journal of Philosophy and Theology* 79, no. 1–2 (2018) 80–104.

Dupré, Louis. *Passage to Modernity: An Essay in the Hermeneutics of Nature and Culture*. New Haven, CT: Yale University Press, 1993.

Falzon, Christopher. "Peter Weir's *The Truman Show* and Sartrean Freedom." In *Existentialism and Contemporary Cinema: A Sartrean Perspective*, edited by Jean-Pierre Boulé and Enda McCaffrey, 17–32. New York: Berghahn, 2011.

Ferrari, Leo. "Beyond Augustine's Conversion Scene." In *Augustine: From Rhetor to Theologian*, edited by Joanne McWilliam, 97–107. Waterloo, ON: Wilfrid Laurier University Press, 1992.

Fifth Lateran Council. "The Human Soul." In *The Sources of Catholic Dogma*, 237–38. Translated by Roy J. Deferrari. St. Louis: B. Herder, 1957.

Fitzpatrick, Joseph. *Philosophical Encounters: Lonergan and the Analytical Tradition*. Toronto: University of Toronto Press, 2005.

Frankfurt, Harry G. *Demons, Dreamers, and Madmen: The Defense of Reason in Descartes's "Meditations."* Princeton, NJ: Princeton University Press, 2008.

Gaukroger, Stephen. *Descartes: An Intellectual Biography*. New York: Oxford University Press, 1995.

Ginascol, Frederick H. "The Question of Universals and the Problem of Faith and Reason." *Philosophical Quarterly* 9, no. 37 (1959) 319–29.

Hatfield, Gary. "Descartes's *Meditations* as Cognitive Exercises." *Philosophy and Literature* 9, no. 1 (1985) 41–58.

——. *The Routledge Guidebook to Descartes' "Meditations."* Abingdon, UK: Routledge, 2014.

Hettche, Matt. "Descartes and the Augustinian Tradition of Devotional Meditation." *Journal of the History of Philosophy* 48, no. 3 (2010) 283–311.

Hughes, Glenn. *Transcendence and History: The Search for Ultimacy from Ancient Societies to Postmodernity.* Columbia: University of Missouri Press, 2003.

Hume, David. *An Enquiry Concerning Human Understanding.* Edited by Peter Millican. Oxford: Oxford University Press, 2007.

Ignatius of Loyola. *The Spiritual Exercises of St. Ignatius.* Translated by Louis Puhl. Chicago: Loyola, 1951.

Johnston, Robert K. "An Exercise in Dialogue: The Movies of Peter Weir." In *Reel Spirituality: Theology and Film in Dialogue*, 2nd ed., 267–90. Grand Rapids: Baker Academic, 2006.

Kalina, Paul. "Designing Visions: Peter Weir & *The Truman Show*." *Cinema Papers* 127 (1998) 18–22 and 56. https://ro.uow.edu.au/cp/127.

Kant, Immanuel. *Critique of Pure Reason.* Translated by Norman Kemp Smith. New York: Palgrave Macmillan, 2007.

Keevak, Michael. "Descartes's Dreams and Their Address for Philosophy." *Journal of the History of Ideas* 53, no. 3 (1992) 373–96.

Kenel, Sally A. *Mortal Gods: Ernest Becker and Fundamental Theology.* Lanham, MD: University Press of America, 1988.

Kenney, John Peter. *Contemplation and Classical Christianity: A Study in Augustine.* Oxford: Oxford University Press, 2013.

Kenny, Anthony. *The Rise of Modern Philosophy.* Oxford: Clarendon, 2006.

King, Darryn. "Director Andrew Niccol Lives in His Own Truman Show (and So Do You)." *Wired*, May 4, 2018. https://www.wired.com/story/director-andrew-niccol-lives-in-the-truman-show.

King, Peter. "Augustine's Anti-Platonist Ascents." In *Augustine's "Confessions": Philosophy in Autobiography*, edited by William E. Mann, 6–27. Oxford: Oxford University Press, 2014.

Knox, Simone. "Reading *The Truman Show* Inside Out." *Film Criticism* 35, no. 1 (2010) 1–23.

Kotzé, Annemaré. *Augustine's "Confessions": Communicative Purpose and Audience.* Leiden: Brill, 2004.

Leonard, Richard. "The Cinematic Mystical Gaze: The Films of Peter Weir." PhD diss., University of Melbourne, 2003. https://hdl.handle.net/11343/38838.

Lewis, James R. *The Astrology Book: The Encyclopedia of Heavenly Influences.* 2nd ed. Canton, MI: Visible Ink, 2003.

Liddy, Richard M. *Transforming Light: Intellectual Conversion in the Early Lonergan.* South Orange, NJ: Bernard Lonergan Institute, 2008. https://works.bepress.com/richard_liddy/32.

Lonergan, Bernard. *Grace and Freedom: Operative Grace in the Thought of St. Thomas Aquinas.* Edited by Frederick E. Crowe and Robert M. Doran. Toronto: University of Toronto Press, 2000.

———. *Insight: A Study of Human Understanding*. 5th ed. Edited by Frederick E. Crowe and Robert M. Doran. Toronto: University of Toronto Press, 1992.

———. *Understanding and Being: The Halifax Lectures on "Insight."* 2nd ed. Edited by Elizabeth A. Murray and Mark D. Morelli. Toronto: University of Toronto Press, 1990.

MacDonald, Paul S. *Descartes and Husserl: The Philosophical Project of Radical Beginnings*. Albany: State University of New York Press, 2000.

———. "Philosophical Conversion." *Philosophy and Theology* 10, no. 2 (1997) 303–27. A revised version of this article appears in MacDonald's *Descartes and Husserl* (see entry above), 225–46. This book quotes from the article since it is more easily obtained.

Mathews, William A. *Lonergan's Quest: A Study of Desire in the Authoring of Insight*. Toronto: University of Toronto Press, 2005.

McMahon, Robert. *Understanding the Medieval Meditative Ascent: Augustine, Anselm, Boethius, and Dante*. Washington, DC: Catholic University of America Press, 2006.

Menn, Stephen. *Descartes and Augustine*. New York: Cambridge University Press, 1998.

Mercadante, Linda A. "The God behind the Screen: *Pleasantville* & *The Truman Show*." *Journal of Religion and Film* 5, no. 2 (2001) 1–17. https://digitalcommons.unomaha.edu/jrf/vol5/iss2/8.

Meynell, Hugo A. *Redirecting Philosophy: Reflections on the Nature of Knowledge from Plato to Lonergan*. Toronto: University of Toronto Press, 1998.

Miles, Margaret R. "On Reading Augustine and on Augustine's Reading." *Christian Century* (May 21–28, 1997) 510–14.

Moleski, Martin X. "Retortion: The Method and Metaphysics of Gaston Isaye." *International Philosophical Quarterly* 17, no. 1 (1977) 59–93.

———. "The Role of Retortion in the Cognitional Analyses of Lonergan and Polanyi." In *Self-Reference: Reflections on Reflexivity*, edited by Steven J. Bartlett and Peter Suber, 218–38. Dordrecht, NL: Martinus Nijhoff, 1987.

Morelli, Mark D. "Going Beyond Idealism: Lonergan's Relation to Hegel." *Lonergan Workshop* 20 (2008) 305–36.

———. *At the Threshold of the Halfway House: A Study of Bernard Lonergan's Encounter with John Alexander Stewart*. Chestnut Hill: Lonergan Institute at Boston College, 2007.

Murray, Elizabeth A. "Bernard Lonergan: An Ignatian Thinker." Paper presented at the Annual Meeting of the American Catholic Philosophical Association, Milwaukee, 2007. https://pje.blog.fordham.edu/wp-content/uploads/2018/03/Murray_Jesuit_ACPA_2007_Lonergan.pdf.

Niccol, Andrew. *"The Truman Show": The Shooting Script*. New York: Newmarket, 1998.

O'Daly, Gerard. *Augustine's Philosophy of Mind*. Berkeley: University of California Press, 1987.

BIBLIOGRAPHY

O'Donnell, James J. *Augustine: A New Biography*. New York: HarperCollins, 2006.

———. *"Confessions": Commentary on Books 1–7*. Oxford: Clarendon, 1992.

Pappas, Nickolas. *Routledge Philosophy Guidebook to Plato and the "Republic."* 2nd ed. New York: Routledge, 2005.

"People Are Alike All Over." Premiered March 25, 1960. *The Twilight Zone: The Complete First Season*. DVD. Hollywood, CA: Paramount, 2016.

Plato. *Republic, Volume II: Books 6–10*. Translated by Paul Shorey. London: William Heinemann, 1935.

Quinn, John M. *A Companion to the "Confessions" of St. Augustine*. New York: Peter Lang, 2002.

Riley, Patrick. *Character and Conversion in Autobiography: Augustine, Montaigne, Descartes, Rousseau, and Sartre*. Charlottesville, VA: University of Virginia Press, 2004.

Saenger, Paul. *Space between Words: The Origins of Silent Reading*. Stanford, CA: Stanford University Press, 1997.

Schwartz, David, et al. *Encyclopedia of TV Game Shows*. 3rd ed. New York: Facts on File, 1999.

Smith, Kurt. *The Descartes Dictionary*. London: Bloomsbury Academic, 2015.

Soranzo, Matteo, and Denis Robichaud. "Philosophical or Religious Conversion? Marsilio Ficino, Plotinus's *Enneads* and Neoplatonic *epistrophê*." In *Simple Twists of "Faith,"* edited by Simona Marchesini and James Nelson Novoa, 135–66. Verona, IT: Alteritas, 2017.

Starnes, Colin. *Augustine's Conversion: A Guide to the Argument of "Confessions" I–IX*. Waterloo, ON: Wilfred Laurier University Press, 1990.

Stohrer, Walter John. "Descartes and Ignatius Loyola: La Flèche and Manresa Revisited." *Journal of the History of Philosophy* 17, no. 1 (1979) 11–27.

Sugden, John. *Sir Francis Drake*. Rev. ed. London: Pimlico, 2006.

The Truman Show. Directed by Peter Weir. Special Edition DVD. Hollywood, CA: Paramount, 2010.

Vaught, Carl G. *Encounters with God in Augustine's "Confessions."* Albany: State University of New York Press, 2004.

Vendler, Zeno. "Descartes' Exercises." *Canadian Journal of Philosophy* 19, no. 2 (1989) 193–224.

Wagner, Stephen I. *Squaring the Circle in Descartes' "Meditations": The Strong Validation of Reason*. Cambridge: Cambridge University Press, 2014.

Weir, Peter. "The Director's Voice." In *Third Take: Australian Film-makers Talk*, edited by Geoff Burton and Raffaele Caputo, 56–64. Crows Nest, NSW: Allen & Unwin, 2002.

Wiebe, Donald. *The Irony of Theology and the Nature of Religious Thought*. Montreal: McGill-Queen's University Press, 1991.

Wills, Garry. *Augustine's "Confessions": A Biography*. Princeton, NJ: Princeton University Press, 2011.

Wilson, Catherine. "Descartes and Augustine." In *A Companion to Descartes*, edited by Janet Broughton and John Carriero, 33–51. Oxford: Blackwell, 2007.